GOING
FOR BROKE

GOING FOR BROKE

HOW ONE OF LATIN AMERICA'S LARGEST FINANCIAL FRAUDS BECAME A BLESSING IN DISGUISE

CARLOS LEGASPY

Published by Advantage, Charleston, South Carolina.
Member of Advantage Media Group.

ADVANTAGE is a registered trademark, and the Advantage colophon is a trademark of Advantage Media Group, Inc.

Printed in the United States of America.

10 9 8 7 6 5 4 3 2 1

ISBN: 978-1-64225-385-6
LCCN: 2022902596

Cover design by David Taylor.
Layout design by Danna Steele.

This publication is designed to provide accurate and authoritative information in regard to the subject matter covered. It is sold with the understanding that the publisher is not engaged in rendering legal, accounting, or other professional services. If legal advice or other expert assistance is required, the services of a competent professional person should be sought.

 Advantage Media Group is proud to be a part of the Tree Neutral® program. Tree Neutral offsets the number of trees consumed in the production and printing of this book by taking proactive steps such as planting trees in direct proportion to the number of trees used to print books. To learn more about Tree Neutral, please visit **www.treeneutral.com.**

Advantage Media Group is a publisher of business, self-improvement, and professional development books and online learning. We help entrepreneurs, business leaders, and professionals share their Stories, Passion, and Knowledge to help others Learn & Grow. Do you have a manuscript or book idea that you would like us to consider for publishing? Please visit **advantagefamily.com**.

To InSight Securities' clients, employees, registered representatives, and investment advisors. You are the reason I was not willing to give up.

To my inner circle, my court of support that held me through it: Myrna Chavira, Jerry Schwartz, James Gaafar, Manlio Arena, and Luis Atristain.

CONTENTS

"If your enemy is secure at all points, be prepared for him. If he is in superior strength, evade him. If your opponent is temperamental, seek to irritate him. Pretend to be weak, that he may grow arrogant. If he is taking his ease, give him no rest. If his forces are united, separate them. If sovereign and subject are in accord, put division between them. Attack him where he is unprepared, appear where you are not expected."

—*Sun Tzu,* The Art of War

FOREWORD

Have you ever felt surrounded, with no visible way out? A situation where, despite your best efforts, everything you had built was slipping through your hands like sand through your fingers? Carlos Legaspy found himself in this very situation in February 2020. He was at the epicenter of the collapse of Biscayne Capital, a firm that had cheated hundreds of Latin American investors of over $300 million of their hard-earned savings.

This is a tale of international finance intrigue combined with some of the best courtroom dramas, but most importantly, it is a deeply spiritual journey in which Carlos had to tap into all of his life experiences—a Mexican immigrant who fought to break into one of the last bastions of white privilege, the good old boy club called Wall Street.

I have known Carlos for years. We are both part of Mankind Project International, and I had a front-row seat to this saga. I saw him cry, saw him rage, and saw him come close to breaking, yet I never saw him want to give up.

This is a classic David versus Goliath story, where international criminals tried to evade their responsibility by pinning it on Carlos. This created a domino effect that brought him to the brink of losing everything. Carlos, in plain language, narrates how he got himself into so much trouble, the things he had to do to survive, and what life lessons he drew from the experience.

The book is full of incredibly colorful characters—so much so that if it were not for the documents that Carlos presents, you could believe they were taken straight out of a comic book or a James Bond movie. As a veteran rugby player, Carlos uses rugby analogies to explain complex aspects of law and finance. This is a must-read for any law student who might want to consider some of Carlos's unorthodox legal strategies.

Join Carlos's adventurer spirit in a journey that will take you from New York to Patagonia, and witness the paradox that at the same time he was fighting some seriously shady characters, some noble people showed up to help Carlos just when he needed it the most.

It is Carlos's hope that his story can help inspire the readers to pursue their dreams, to transcend whatever limitations they believe they have.

Mariano W. Guas Jr., DVM
Full Leader
Mankind Project International

INTRODUCTION

The Cañon de Guadalupe is a landscape of striking contrasts: Edenic waterfalls, soothing hot springs, and patches of lush vegetation spring up among the vast, parched desert of Baja California, Mexico. It is a place of great beauty in all its extremes, from the life-giving natural springs that crisscross the land and the palm trees and desert flowers to the brilliant but hellish sun, which also gives life—but can take it away from travelers who don't respect the ferocity of this parched climate. Nature is as comforting as it is unforgiving.

I was enjoying the majestic beauty of this land with my friend Richard during a camping trip in 2012. We had driven down from San Diego for the weekend. I was familiar with the area, having visited several times before, but the place never failed to make an impression on me.

In our rented jeep, Richard and I tooled along the long dirt road that led to the campsite fifty miles away. The track was uneven and eroded, and even with our rugged four-wheel-drive vehicle, the ridged, washboard-like surface made for a slow and bumpy ride.

I knew of an alternate route across the expansive dry lake bed that sprawled alongside the road. I had taken it several times before. It was flat and barren—nothing but dust and sediment left from the ancient body of water that had dried up eons ago. But because it was so flat, it made for easier, faster driving than tediously navigating the dirt road.

So we turned off the road and headed toward the horizon, following the tracks left by other vehicles that had made the same detour. After cruising along for a while, admiring the view, suddenly the jeep struck an unseen sandbar. We lurched forward, unable to go any farther, as the jeep's front wheels spun helplessly in the air.

Richard and I got out to assess the situation as the sun beat down on our backs. Evidently, someone had been digging a trench across the middle of the lake bed, forming an impassable barrier, with no warning signs to alert unaware motorists. Our efforts to dislodge the vehicle were unsuccessful. We were stuck, immobilized in the sand.

A dry lake bed is a desolate landscape, awesome in the literal sense of the word: it inspires awe, a feeling of immensity, dread, and wonder. That part of the Cañon de Guadalupe is like Luke Sky-walker's barren homestead of Tatooine. There was nothing around, not even a piece of wood to stick under the tires to gain traction. And there was not a soul in sight. No cell phone signal either. It was 11:00 a.m., and the sun was already menacing. It was threatening to be a blistering day.

I was no stranger to crisis at that point in my life, and neither Richard nor I was prone to panic, so we stayed calm despite the gravity of the situation. After it became clear that there was no way to dislodge the jeep from the sandbar, we just waited there in the hope that another vehicle would traverse the lake bed. But no one was coming for us.

We had driven too long and were too far from the original road to turn back on foot. But I knew there was another road that ran parallel to the first one. Our only hope was to set out on foot and try to reach the other road, which we estimated would take an hour or two of walking, though we had no clue how far it actually was or if we would even be able to make it. We were basically staking our lives on the accuracy of that guess. We weren't naive: we knew the open desert can kill you. It is not a good place to tempt fate.

Nevertheless, all out of options, we grabbed as much water as we could from the jeep and set off across the dusty expanse of the lake bed toward the wall of a mountain that rose up behind the horizon.

An hour passed with no road in sight. Then two hours. It was 120 degrees with no shade, and our water was dwindling. What at first was a worrying but remote possibility was quickly turning into a terrifying likelihood. A grim, unspoken question loomed in our minds: "What if we don't make it?"

Besides Richard and me, and a few straggly bushes and desert scrub pummeled by the wind, the only thing remotely resembling a life-form in that landscape was the sun, which burned with a fierce, unrelenting intensity, like a big fiery eye in the sky. Watching us. Challenging us. Daring us to survive its wrath.

In such moments, when faced with an impossible task or insurmountable odds, there will be part of you that is tempted to give up, give in. To stop fighting. We were growing tired and weary, and it could have been easy to tell ourselves, "Let's just stop here and wait. Maybe someone has found our jeep by now and called out a rescue team."

But a louder, clearer voice in my head said, "Carlos, if you stop walking, you're going to die."

And though we were gambling with our lives by forging ahead in search of the road, the choice was clear. If I'm going down, I'm going down fighting. At least this way we'd have a chance.

> Though we were gambling with our lives by forging ahead in search of the road, the choice was clear. If I'm going down, I'm going down fighting.

That thought kept me going.

We pressed on in silence, both of us wrestling with the possibility that we might not make it. Our bodies cried out for water to slake our fearsome thirst. I thought of the many migrants from Mexico and Central America who never make it to the end of the long trek across the desert—they get dehydrated, they lose the route or misestimate the distance, and the sun and earth swallow them whole. The bodies of many of these unfortunate souls are never discovered. They just become part of the landscape that killed them.

I thought of the people I loved, my family. I hadn't actually told anyone I was making this trip, so no one even knew I was there.

Strangely, I was not panicking. In fact, as the situation grew direr, I felt a sense of peace and acceptance. This is different from giving up. Giving up is ceasing the fight. Surrender is accepting the reality of what is, recognizing that some things are simply out of your hands. *This is my time—thank you for a great life.* There was no self-pity, no "woe is me." Everybody has to go sometime, I thought. Paradoxically, there is a certain empowerment in that act of acceptance.

By now we had been walking four hours. Our water was long gone, but at least there were a few squat, scraggly desert plants that were big enough to provide a little shade. We would rest under there and gather our strength before pressing on.

I tried not to fixate on it, but the specter of death was always there, like a third person, walking closely behind us. I kept my gaze fixed ahead, on the purple mountain and the blue sky behind it. The unseen road I knew was somewhere out there. Our only hope.

Finally, around 5:00 p.m., after six miserable hours of walking, we spotted a car cruising across the lake bed. Like castaways lost on some desert island who spot a distant ship, we waved and shouted frantically. The driver was too far to see us, but we knew now that rescue was imminent. We had found the other road.

Soon, we reached it. The sun was finally starting to dip down behind the mountain range. We were on the road, but the vista before us was completely desolate. No one in sight. We hoped someone would come. Hopefully before nightfall.

We waited an hour until we saw an approaching VW Golf. As it pulled up beside us, we saw it was packed full of gear and people. It was a *National Geographic* crew filming a documentary about the local wildlife. A woman got out and took stock of these two parched wanderers who were ecstatic about being found. "We can't take you with us, but we'll get you help," she said.

We sat by a bush and waited as they drove on. The setting sun cast everything in a warm, heavenly glow. An hour passed, and we started to wonder again if something had gone wrong—if the crew had gotten waylaid or whoever they had sent to help us had gotten the wrong message about our location. But finally, we saw a man and a dog walking toward us.

The man introduced himself as Mario, the groundskeeper of a nearby ranch. Mario was lean and wiry, with the tanned, creased face befitting a ranch hand.

After being alerted by the *National Geographic* crew, he walked three miles to retrieve us, and we followed him on foot back to his ranch as the light faded into the deep black night. When we arrived, he pumped out water from the well, and seeing the cold, crystalline liquid spring forth was like heaven. We munched on some bread he gave us and felt instantly better.

"Six hours is a long time to be out there," Mario told me in Spanish. "You are lucky to be alive."

"I know," I said. But I knew that luck was only part of it.

I offered money to thank him but he refused, though I'm sure he had very little of it himself. "You don't do favors for money," he said.

Later, Mario borrowed a truck and some chains, and we drove back to the sandbar in the lake bed, where we were able to pull the jeep free. As we began driving back, we saw the solitary glow of a single flashlight, and soon a man was emblazoned by the headlights of our jeep. He had a wild, anxious look on his face, a look we certainly recognized as he, too, had been driving across the lake bed with his family when his car got stuck. So we were able to free him too.

When my return flight to San Diego crossed over the same desert and I was able to look down at the lake bed, that's really when it hit me how hostile and expansive that place is and how close we had come to dying out there.

That experience changed my life. It taught me some great lessons about how small and fragile we humans are—and how big and resilient we are too. Sometimes we fight over the most insignificant things, while the world spins around us and people struggle with existential conflicts—sometimes the literal life-and-death conflicts of physical survival, sometimes life-and-death struggles over the soul. Sometimes we get consumed by the pursuit of money and success, and meanwhile a ranch hand who owns next to nothing would journey into the night to rescue a stranger and refuse to accept a reward for his good deed.

Life can be beautiful, but it can also be a knockdown, drag-out battle royal. There are periods where as soon as you vanquish one foe, another will be charging at you with his fist cocked back, ready to swing. My near-fatal trip through the desert was a valuable learning experience that in many ways presaged the ordeal of the last several years, when, through my work as a broker-dealer, I uncovered a massive Ponzi scheme—and ended up getting accused of malfeasance and fraud by various individuals who tried to pin the blame on me instead.

In the chapters to come, I'll take you inside that crisis and tell you how I went toe to toe with big investment banks, international hustlers, opportunistic attorneys, and predatory regulatory authorities to come back from the brink of financial and professional ruin.

What I have learned is that I can either shut down, go bankrupt, wither and fade away—or I can fight back. I can either try to go it alone, or I can open, be vulnerable, and ask for help when I know I need it. I can swallow my pride. I can accept the reality of failure and not be ashamed of it but instead accept that every great success story is, on closer inspection, made up of many smaller failures along the way. I imagine that it is part of some divine plan that God, the universe, fate, or whatever word you prefer has for each of us. Just as there was a reason Richard and I got lost that day.

I have always been a fighter, *un luchador*, and I know my near-death experience in the desert hardened me even more against surrender and gave me the additional confidence to survive the battles to come. I hope my story will imbue you with the same spirit.

CHAPTER 1

THE DARKEST HOUR

The stress was mounting, so I went for a walk.

It was February 2020, and I was strolling alongside Lake Michigan. The lake in winter is a sight to behold. The beaches, which teem with people during the summer, are quiet. The cold wind whipping off the lake reaches all the way into your bones. It has an austere beauty, and the chill invigorates you, makes you awake and alive. That evening, the lights sparkled on the surface and glinted off the chunks of ice that had formed in the subzero weather. It was going to be a long, hard winter for me. I thought of spring and, picturing the lake with the ice gone and the flowers in bloom, hoped my situation would improve by then.

By the end of 2019, I was in big trouble—swimming in a sea full of sharks while a tidal wave of legal problems was breaking over me. I had been accused of fraud by clients who had lodged six complaints with the Financial Industry Regulatory Authority (FINRA), the private body that oversees brokers. Six complaints totaling $40 million. Those individuals had been victimized—not by me but by their own unscrupulous financial advisors, who held their accounts at my firm, InSight Securities. And now those same advisors were plotting with their own bamboozled clients to shift the blame onto me.

The whole affair was the culmination of a bizarre turn of events that started with me blowing the whistle on a Ponzi scheme run by a company that my firm had been providing services to, a scandal that impacted some of the biggest players in the financial industry.

As anyone who has been to the brink can attest, one crisis tends to snowball into the next. With all this controversy swirling around me, Pershing LLC, my financial clearing company for many years, abruptly terminated our business relationship, spooked by all the allegations against me, even if they were unproven. A broker-dealer such as myself cannot operate without an agreement with the clearing house, which confirms, settles, and delivers transactions. It's like if I were the owner of a Ford dealership. I make money selling Ford's cars and servicing its vehicles. But if one day Ford comes to me and says, "We don't want you using our name anymore," I'm done for.

A Ford auto dealer who can't sell Ford products is effectively out of business.

Following that, the claim I lodged with our litigation insurance company was denied. For a broker, such insurance covers a lot of things; for example, say you purchase securities on behalf of a client, the securities tank (through no fault or foreknowledge of your own), and the client, blaming you for a bad bet, takes you to court. That's not a case the client would likely win, but in any event, your litigation insurance will offer you

> A Ford auto dealer who can't sell Ford products is effectively out of business.

protection in the ensuing civil action. Unfortunately for me, the claim was denied for technical reasons.

Things were imploding rapidly. FINRA complaints are public information before they go to hearing so there isn't presumption of innocence in the public eye, and now that my name was tied to major accusations of malfeasance, no one wanted to work with me. I couldn't find another clearing firm, and winning new business in this climate was out of the question. It was like the floor beneath my feet was crumbling, leaving me hanging over an abyss. My thirty-year career was about to go up in smoke, and I hadn't done anything wrong.

The Background

How did I end up in this unenviable situation? There are two antagonists in this story (among several others), whom you will come to know well. The first is an Ecuadorian woman named Edith Hinojosa, who was the number one salesperson for a now-disgraced investment firm called Biscayne Capital. I provided services to two companies called Total and Pro Advisors, which were the successors, through a convoluted sham sale, of Biscayne, by holding $160 million in securities Edith had purchased on behalf of her clients. My company and I, of course, had no clue these securities were bogus. They were being priced and were making their scheduled interest payments. We were merely executing our usual custodial duties as a third party.

Eventually, these notes became worthless, and we started fielding frantic, angry calls from Edith's clients when they realized their investments had tanked. Instead of directing their ire (and their legal firepower) on the culpable parties, the clients, at Edith's incitement, sued *us*.

Meanwhile, another fraudster, Fernando Haberer, was engaged in a similar scheme, selling the same worthless notes to his own clients.

As the scheme started to circle the drain, he needed to park these notes somewhere, and by then we had restricted its trading. Since he couldn't park them with us, he parked them at Deutsche Bank. He ended up overdrafting his client's account there by $12.3 million, and to rectify that overdrafted account, he orchestrated a plan in which he gave us fraudulent instructions to transfer money out of *his* customers' accounts (at our brokerage) to Deutsche Bank.

Once the Biscayne / Total / Pro Advisers scheme imploded, causing multiple clients to lose millions in savings, I ended up being the fall guy. I was basically framed. All of a sudden I was facing an avalanche of legal claims.

And thus enters another antagonist that would come to make my life miserable for several years: the Financial Industry Regulatory Authority, better known as FINRA. Every broker-dealer by law must be signatory to FINRA, which is not actually a government agency but a private entity designed to keep brokers and brokerage firms' noses clean. A worthwhile goal in theory, since the industry needs a mechanism to enforce regulations, but in practice, there is a lot wrong with FINRA, not least of which is the fact that the way it operates creates a hostile environment for defendants, like me, who are hit with baseless complaints.

One of the conditions of being a FINRA member is agreeing to arbitration to resolve disputes. Contrast this with a lawsuit adjudicated in the civil court system, where the usual rights and norms of due process prevail. In FINRA hearings, there is no presumption of innocence, arbitrators are not required to follow the law, lying is not sanctioned as perjury and there are many problems with arbitration generally: it is less transparent than the civil judicial system, there is little or no recourse to appeal a decision, and vast power is vested in the arbitrator (who may be poorly trained) rather than a jury of your peers or a judge.

Unfortunately, because brokers are legally beholden to the vagaries of arbitration, there is now a cottage industry of financial "ambulance chasers," lawyers who are looking to put the squeeze on brokers, knowing that arbitration is not always fair and that brokers who are working to come out from under the shadow of an open complaint often succumb to the pressure and settle for vast amounts of money, even when they didn't do anything wrong.

In the darkest days of this crisis, I felt like Thelma and Louise in that famous climactic scene of the movie: boxed in, chased from all directions, a desperado in the desert, with no way out except by driving off the precipice into the canyon below.

I remembered how that film ended. I prayed the outcome would be different for me.

As I pondered how grave things seemed, the same profound mix of emotions that I experienced in the windswept wilds of Baja California came over me. There was intense fear, like I was looking at the end—not the end of my life this time but the destruction of my business, my career, and my reputation. But pushing back against that feeling of dread was acceptance, combined with a will to fight. I would do everything in my power to clear my name and get back on my feet. But if I were to ultimately lose that fight, I would surrender to my fate, recognizing that some things are simply out of your hands.

Just like that life-changing day in the Cañon de Guadalupe, I set my sights on the mountain in the distance and marched on. If I was going down, it wasn't going to be because I stopped trying. And at that moment of acceptance—of the reality, of the challenge—I dug in.

CHAPTER 2

A KID FROM JUÁREZ

Juárez is a city that appears regularly in the headlines these days, and mostly for the wrong reasons. But there is much more to this dusty border town than the crime and chaos with which it is often associated. It's a genuine and hardworking community with its own rugged charisma, and, as the place where I grew up, it shaped the man I am today.

Juárez is a place on the margins. It sits right on the southwestern boundary of the United States, the second-busiest border crossing. Growing up, we could practically see downtown El Paso, Texas, from our front yard. Given its liminal geography, Juárez has always had a transient, dynamic quality owing to the large numbers of Mexican emigrants heading to the United States, the arrival of poor Mexicans from the southern region of Mexico venturing north for work, and a constant flow of American and Mexican citizens moving back and forth across the border. Not just people but capital and goods move between the two cities, as Juárez epitomizes the close, if often fraught, economic relationship Mexico shares with the United States.

We *juarenses* were and are pragmatic people. We dealt with racism and discrimination that occurred when crossing the border, but it didn't deter us. El Paso and Juárez are like stepsiblings—born of different parents but bonded by a fraternal spirit. And you can't keep stepsiblings apart for long.

It was easier when I was growing up to cross the border. When I was a teenager, sometimes we'd go into El Paso to meet friends, bring them back to Mexico for a party, and then drive over again and drop them off at their homes in Texas. So I grew up with a bicultural perspective.

Other Mexicans tend to see Juárez as a very Americanized city, a metropolis with little of the cultural and aesthetic charm for which Mexico, with its pre-Columbian ruins, beautiful old churches, colonial architecture, and whitewashed beaches, is admired. It's an industrial (and industrious) city in the high desert, where the Rio Grande (or the *Rio Bravo del Norte*, as it is known there) drifts lazily but powerfully by. Ceaseless, eternal, never stopping.

These qualities imbue Juárez with a certain dynamism, even a restless quality. Perhaps on some level that's why I, too, have always felt on the move, whether professionally or geographically—upward in pursuit of big career goals or across the land in search of a new place to call home.

You could say that I became familiar with the porous boundary between El Paso, USA, and Ciudad Juárez, Mexico, from a very young age—the first time I traversed the border, I was still in my momma's belly, all set to begin my journey on earth. My mother traveled to Texas shortly before my birth so that I would have US citizenship, which she knew would afford me more opportunities if I eventually chose to live in the United States. I guess she had the right idea, since I'm still here!

My own life story, as you can probably already gather, has been anything but conventional, and my parents were the same way. They deviated from the norm and carved their own path. My mom was young when she started dating my father, and I was an unplanned pregnancy, which in 1960s Mexico was quite a scandal—the kind of news that would make your pious *tía* faint and have your straitlaced *tío* running for the smelling salts to revive her. Things have become a little more relaxed since then, but the expectations in the conservative Catholic country at the time was that a young couple "in trouble" would get married immediately and be "legitimate" by the time their baby came into the world.

My parents decided against that. They didn't want to get married just to conform to some old-fashioned social mores. But they were pragmatic, and they understood that, young as they were, they were not in an ideal position to raise a child. So together they agreed that I would be raised by my maternal grandparents.

It was very much a nontraditional family structure, but what we lacked in tradition we made up for in love.

My grandparents had an interesting story of their own. My grandmother was born in 1926. She was stunningly beautiful and married at fourteen. My grandfather was eight years older, the eldest son of a military man who fought in the Mexican Revolution and settled in Juárez after the Mexican Civil War.

My grandfather, a handsome, fair-skinned man with a thin 1940s-style mustache, was a rebel compared to his strict, martial father. He was all about living life, seeking adventure, and traveling. I inherited that adventurousness from him (as well as the name "Carlos"). When I was a boy, the three of us traveled all over the country in a camper he built from scratch. He was also a man of his times, *machista,* and had many affairs on the side, but he loved my grandma dearly. And she loved him just as passionately.

My grandparents did not advance past elementary school, but they understood the value of education and encouraged me to do well in school. They made up for their lack of formal schooling with an entrepreneurial drive, and by the time I was born, my grandfather owned a couple junkyards, which afforded us a comfortable middle-class existence.

I'd see my father from time to time growing up, but he eventually married someone else and started his own family. I never really had a relationship with my father, but this was okay. It wasn't a source of hardship or trauma or anything like that; he just wasn't a major part of my life.

My mother, too, eventually married. And my grandmother, who was still pretty young herself, had a daughter two years after I was born. She was technically my aunt but more like a baby sister.

While my grandfather held things down on the business front, my *abuela* was the CEO of the family—a true matriarch. I was raised by strong women: my grandma, my aunts, and, of course, my mother. Although my mom didn't live under the same roof, she resided nearby and played a big role in my upbringing.

Both Mom and Grandma were, as I said, very nontraditional. They weren't hippies exactly but "hippie-ish." Easygoing, open minded, and nonjudgmental, they flagrantly and joyfully flouted the restrictive mores of the time. For example, when one of my unmarried cousins got pregnant, they all thought it was great and happily told their friends the news that in other families would have been met with hushed whispers and embarrassed attempts to hide it.

I think this nonreligious, untraditional environment encouraged my free-thinking nature. Ironically, I did attend Catholic school, but this was just my mom's way of exposing me to different viewpoints. "Believe in whatever you want. It's your choice," she said. I've tried to live by that credo ever since.

From the Junkyard to Junk Bonds

My grandparents owned a big house outside the city. When I was born, we had no neighbors and were surrounded by cotton fields. Tumbleweed would sometimes drift by. In the mornings, the crisp smell of the desert rose up from the damp earth. The closest neighbors—friends of mine—lived on the other side of an irrigation canal, which was passable only by walking over some flimsy wooden boards, and I remember the act of crossing over felt exhilarating, like leaving one realm and entering a new one.

I think I was born with a natural predilection for adventure seeking, and for such a child, it was the perfect place to be—lots of room to explore. I was always eager to "see what's on the other side." I still am. So I would spend hours roaming the fields nearby, to see how far I could get before I had to turn back. Unlike some overprotective mothers, my mom encouraged this exploratory spirit. "Just be careful!" she said.

> I think I was born with a natural predilection for adventure seeking.

Eventually the city grew and grew, basically doubling in size in just twenty years until it engulfed our neighborhood. No more tumbleweed and cotton fields. By the time I was in high school, Juárez was fully urbanized.

As the city expanded, the family business expanded with it. My grandfather sourced cars from all over the area and would frequently cross into the United States to buy more. He was lighter complected, with hair the color of ripe wheat, and when he traveled around rural Texas, he came face-to-face with the ugliness of Jim Crow—often, he wasn't even allowed to sit with his darker-skinned workers.

In the yard, we would fix up old cars and sell them to used-car lots, or if it was a lost cause, we'd strip it for parts. After school, I worked alongside my grandfather, surrounded on all sides by mountains of radiators and alternators and old tires.

This upbringing provided a valuable education in all things mechanical. As a kid, I'd build "robots" from spare parts lying around, and I learned to drive at age eleven, moving vehicles around the yard. One day an old 1963 AMC Rambler came in, and Grandpa said, "If you can fix it, it's yours." That was my first car.

By the time I reached middle school, I didn't want to deal with the nuns anymore, so I transferred to public school. I brought my predilection for building and tinkering into the classroom, where I signed up for a shop class, and did well in my studies of electronics and radio. By the time I got to high school, I expected my future career would be in something like engineering or electronics.

This was in the early '80s, around the start of the home computing revolution that would completely alter how we all live and work. My father bought me a Commodore 64, that boxy gray eight-bit machine with a paltry sixty-four kilobytes of memory—a device that today you are more likely to see in a museum than in an office. But at the time, it was state of the art. And this early exposure to computing helped inspire an interest in pursuing computer science in college.

My high school was also a public school, a somewhat shabby building on the outskirts of the city. I was elected student body president, and one of my big initiatives was organizing fundraisers for the underfunded school. This caught the eye of the local Rotary Club, which invited me to their youth leadership program, where they would identify young go-getters, invite them on retreats and trainings, and pair them with mentors.

The Rotary Club's youth leadership events, in turn, attracted the attention of recruiters at Monterrey Tech, a prestigious private university that had just opened a campus in Juárez. From the recruiters, I learned that Monterrey Tech had a program that combined business and computer science, which was right up my alley. I applied and was awarded a scholarship, and that's how I got into "the MIT of Mexico."

A funny thing about life is that sometimes, one stroke of luck begets another, and, as if by fate, things slide into place. It's like hitting six green lights in a row when you're cruising down a busy street—just in a bigger, more cosmic sense. My school fundraising schemes had led to mentorship by the Rotary Club, which brought me into the orbit of the university recruiters, which landed me in this coveted scholarship program—and that, in turn, would bring me into contact with a young professor who would change the course of my life.

That man was Federico Esquivel, a visiting professor who also worked for one of the industrial park developers in the city—one of the *maquiladoras* that produced parts for American factories over the border. Federico was a tall man who looked, well, like what you'd think an economist would look like. An academic type, with thick economist glasses.

In the second semester of my freshman year, I was enrolled in his economics course, and for our final project for the semester, we had to design a country from scratch, replete with a bespoke form of government, an economic system, all of that. Even with my computer background, in those days, we were still using typewriters to write our papers, so the version you handed in was usually the sole existing copy.

Federico posted the exam grades on the door and left the graded papers with the receptionist, but mine was missing. I really wanted my graded copy, so I drove to his office in Juárez.

"You said you'd leave the papers there, but they're not there, and I'd like my copy back, please," I said.

"Yours is there. Go tell the secretary to look for it. But now that you're here, what are you doing this summer?"

"I don't know," I said. "Hanging out?"

"Would you like to work for me?"

"Sure!" I said, jumping at the chance. "What do you guys actually do?"

He laughed and proceeded to fill me in on the job. Federico was the VP of financial planning, and the company was using a new software, Lotus 123, for its bookkeeping. But no one there actually knew how to operate it, and since he knew I had some computing expertise, I would be a good fit for the role.

I ended up working there for a year, and the experience was my first up-close look at the world of finance, which of course ended up being my future—though I did not know it at the time.

In 1987, at age twenty, it was time to make the move to the main campus in Monterrey, as required by the scholarship program. Monterrey is a good twenty hours over land from Juárez—needless to say, much farther than I'd ever been from home in my life. My mom and my grandma cried in the next room as I packed my bags. No one in my family had ever attended college or even left town. It was a big moment for all of us.

From the first day, I could tell that Monterrey had a different flavor. Unlike the dry desert air of Juárez, it was hot and humid, with a climate similar to Houston's. Though it was much larger than Juárez, it had a conservative, small-town mentality that made me miss my more liberal hometown, with its wilder nightlife, access to American television, and the bilingual culture of the borderland.

The scholarship covered tuition but not living expenses. And while my grandparents had done well most of their lives, they were suffering from the effects of the Latin American financial crisis that started in 1982 and had severely devalued the peso. They had always supported me growing up. But I was determined to not be a burden on them now.

Hunger is a great motivator, and I got to looking for work. I came across a want ad for a reporter who could cover science and technology for *El Norte*, a renowned local newspaper. I figured it was a long shot—I had no professional journalism experience—but it just felt "right," a kind of "Spidey sense" that compelled me to pursue it. Then as now, I probably had a surplus of confidence. Overconfidence is a blessing as well as a curse, but it has always encouraged me to embrace activities outside of my comfort zone. And I liked the ego boost of seeing my name in a byline: "by Carlos Legaspy." Anyway, what was the worst that could happen?

Against the odds, my application was accepted, and I quickly settled into the role, which gave me the chance to interview prominent people in the tech sector. I wrote about how Steve Jobs got kicked out of Apple and about the first computer virus that ravaged global computing networks. I made my own hours and was able to juggle classes and homework, interviewing folks between class and going to the paper office to write my stories. It was a cool gig.

That lasted until 1989, when I went home for the summer, the last break before graduation.

I was in the supermarket one afternoon when I ran into my old professor Federico, who was searching a pile of cantaloupes for a ripe one. We caught up on what we were doing: I told him I would be finishing my degree in six months, and he said he was now working for a brokerage firm. His money market trader had just quit and his replacement wouldn't be joining for another three months, so they needed someone to fill the gap.

"We really need to fill his seat. Do you want to do it?"

"Sure!" I said. "What's a money market trader?"

He smiled. "Come to the office, and I'll explain it to you."

Mexico, as I mentioned, was in the throes of hyperinflation. But the nature of capitalism is that, for better or worse, the flip side of a crisis is an opportunity. There was a big business in investing money overnight at huge interest rates just to keep pace with inflation, and that's what I'd be doing.

"See those phones on the wall?" Federico said. "Those connect to the main desk in Mexico City. And the client will tell you whether they're looking for money or they're looking to invest. If it's money they want, the cheaper you can get it, the more we make. If they have money and want to invest, the better return you get for them, the more we make. Can you do that?"

"Absolutely," I said. Of course I had no clue what he was talking about, and even once I started working I didn't know what I was doing, but I quickly figured it out. The haggling skills I had picked up all those years working with my grandfather in the junkyard served me well. "Imagine that," said Federico. "You went from junk cars to junk bonds!"

I excelled enough in the role that they offered me a permanent position, which I agreed to accept following completion of my studies in Monterrey.

During the final semester, one day when walking to my morning class, I spotted on the same bulletin board where I saw the newspaper job ad another notice for an international exchange program run by AIESEC. AIESEC has chapters worldwide and partners with companies all over the globe to arrange paid internships for foreign students. It's normally a competitive program, but that year they had more jobs than applicants, so they were eager for fresh talent.

I applied, noting on the application that I would be willing to be sent pretty much anywhere, for any length of time. Some of my friends threw their hat in the ring too.

Months passed. Some of them were posted to Madrid; another was Tokyo bound—but I hadn't heard anything. I still had the brokerage job awaiting me at least.

Then, graduation happened, and I packed up and drove back home, disappointed my application hadn't been accepted. Finally, one day my grandma answered the phone and said, "Carlos! There's an American woman on the phone for you!" She hadn't understood a word of what the English-speaking caller was saying. But I knew immediately who was on the other end of the line.

AIESEC had found me a spot with a New York firm, and I accepted. I went back to my old professor and humbly thanked him for holding open the position at the brokerage but said this opportunity was too valuable to turn down. He agreed.

"I went to school in NY. Got my master's at Columbia. You're going to love it."

I sold my truck to buy a plane ticket, packed my belongings, and tied up loose ends. If my mom and grandma were sad to see me off to Monterrey, you can imagine how they felt about their boy jetting off to New York. My grandmother had the hardest time of my relatives saying goodbye. I was practically a son to her.

Every endeavor, every adventure, I've lived with the ethos to never give up—keep going until they stop you. This was no different, and I knew I had my mom's support too. Fortune favors the bold, she believed, and she instilled in me the confidence for this next adventure.

> Every endeavor, every adventure, I've lived with the ethos to never give up—keep going until they stop you.

"You can always come back if you fail," she said. "But you won't."

I left Mexico on Friday, February 2, 1990, for El Paso, where I was flying from. February 5 is a holiday in Mexico, so the line to cross the international bridge was unusually long, and a snowfall was adding to the chaos.

Between the long line and the stack of immigration paperwork to fill out, I nearly missed my flight. American Airlines was holding the gate open as I was running down the hallway, and security radioed that I was on my way. There was no time for goodbyes; I kissed my mom and grandmother and hopped on the plane, grateful that my rushed exit left no time for tears at the gate.

Catching my breath once I found my seat on the plane, it hit me: "What the fuck am I doing?" I felt fear for the first time.

But for a thrill seeker, the flip side of fear is exhilaration. And that's what keeps you going. It was time to cross to the other side and see what was out there.

CHAPTER 3

FROM WALL STREET TO ALAMO CITY

One of the things I've always admired about my mom is her pragmatic resilience. When she got pregnant, she considered me a gift from God even though giving birth to a child out of wedlock was taboo. Instead of being ashamed, she embraced it proudly, because she understood that in life, you have to make your own way, even if that means fighting for it or going against the grain.

That was a lesson she imparted to me early on. One of my earliest childhood memories is of running around outside and tripping and falling hard. I burst into tears. My grandmother went to pick me up, but my mother waved her off. Instead, she crouched down next to me and said, "Carlos, you can pick yourself up." She knew she would not always be around to protect me and wanted to teach me how to survive in the world.

Now, all those lessons from childhood, adolescence, and young adulthood were being tested. And there is no bigger, badder arena to test your mettle than New York City—especially in the epicenter of cutthroat, sink-or-swim ambition: Wall Street.

Before arriving in New York, my only visits to the United States were trips to El Paso and brief visits to Los Angeles to see family. I didn't even *know* anyone who had been to New York City. I only knew it from the movies. I didn't know what a bagel was. I had never seen a taxi driver wearing a turban. I was, admittedly, a provincial kid. But it was all a thrill. And as provincial as I may have been, I was ready to take on the world.

Before I started my career on Wall Street proper, I did my AIESEC internship at IBM. There were about thirty of us in the program from all over the world, and I relished the cornucopia of cultures into which I was immersed. I shared an apartment with an Indian guy and a Greek girl, and our circle of friends included people from Denmark, Malaysia, all over the place.

I worked for IBM for a full year before the next opportunity arose, thanks to—who else?—Federico Esquivel. The company he was working for, Banca Serfin, had opened up an office in New York. Federico was coming to New York to run it, and he needed an assistant.

I helped him get acclimated to the city, but Federico's tenure in New York was brief. He never quite felt at home there, and the job wasn't a good fit either. He got into a big fight with his boss and requested a transfer back to Juárez, and I took over his position.

From assistant to senior account executive in just a matter of months.

The work was as enthralling as the city. Math, strategy, high stakes—the perfect combination for a young, ambitious risk-taker who wanted to learn and make a name for himself. At first there were only five of us, a small team doing big things. We were the first Mexican brokerage in the States, and we were pretty much making it up as we went along. That is the sort of challenge that I have embraced during my long career in finance. When I'm starting from scratch and have to build everything from the ground up, that's when I'm happiest.

It was a period of fervent economic expansion in Mexico. Changes in the regulatory landscape opened up new opportunities in all sectors, and there were numerous IPOs of Mexican companies. We were in the right place at the right time—little did we know it would all come crashing to a halt in a few years when the Mexican economy took a nosedive. But such is the nature of finance. You go along with the economic ebb and flow and try to keep your boat afloat.

I managed a team that serviced as advisors in different parts of Mexico that had their clients. We were in the business of selling, with a manifold product portfolio: stocks, insurance, mutual funds, etc. The company was something of a financial supermarket. Mostly we were selling to other salespeople, which required a lot of creativity: How do you convince salespeople to sell your product over others?

I found that sales came naturally to me, and I enjoyed coming up with tricks and techniques to get an edge. For example, I chuckle now when recalling how when a broker in Mexico would make a big sale and earn a big commission from our products, I would fax them a confirmation of the trade. I knew that this incoming fax would likely be seen by other people in his or her office as it sat in the tray waiting to be picked up. Sometimes I'd even send it "by mistake" to other branches so that the brokers there would see how much brokers working with *us* were making, in the hopes they'd pick up the phone and say, "Hey, I want in. I want to sell your products too."

For a skinny kid of twenty-four years old (but who looked sixteen), I did pretty well and handled myself with confidence. Fortunately, we did virtually everything on the phone, which probably saved me from losing deals from my baby-faced appearance. It was quite a long time before we actually met in person any of the Mexican advisors we worked with. When we finally *did* meet, one of them looked at me and said, "Lucky for you we did business over the phone because if I had met you, I never would have bought anything from you!"

"The Son of My Father"

It wouldn't be a proper story about Wall Street without an account of the dark side.

My time at the bank wasn't all fun and games. As the office grew in size, the friendship and camaraderie of the early days ebbed, and I had to deal with a lot of backstabbing and bigotry, which reminded me that even while working for a Mexican bank, a self-made Mexican guy with an unconventional upbringing was not really accepted as "part of the club." It was a very WASP-y and/or Jewish kind of old boys' network, and if you didn't fit in with either of those groups, you weren't accepted as an equal.

The hostility I faced wasn't usually overt. It took the form of subtle, disparaging, or dismissive comments or attitudes—what we know today as "microaggressions," though that wasn't a term in my or most people's vocabulary back then. But they were no less damaging.

In hindsight, I think I had a certain naivete that made me oblivious to a lot of it. There were things that were said and done that I felt were innocuous but in fact were offensive. And English is not my first language, so some of the linguistic nuances went over my head. For example, it was sometimes hard for me to detect sarcasm, which added a complicated wrinkle to office conversations or after-work socializing. And as much as I was integrated in the fabric of New York life, I was still perceived as a foreigner.

Even among Mexicans, I was regarded as an outsider since I was a middle-class kid from Juárez and not from the aristocratic elite of Mexico City—people who came from generational wealth, the upper crust. In the company, you were judged less by your own merit than by your family pedigree. A common question would be "And whose son are you?" The implication being that your father's worth determined your own. "I am the son of my father, and I'm here because I worked hard to get here" was my answer to this question, and I said it with pride. But it wasn't really an attitude they respected.

As the New York office expanded and new employees were added to the ranks (mostly from the same WASP-y, Jewish, or rich Mexican milieu), I observed that many new hires were chosen only because their dad served on the board of some blue-chip corporation or had family connections from some private golf club in the affluent environs of *la Ciudad de México*.

What really got under my skin was not so much that certain people didn't like me for my background—that I could deal with—

but that they were often dismissive of my *ideas* because I wasn't part of the club. I'd come with a proposal, they'd reject it, and then someone else would pitch the same idea and they'd go ahead with it. No matter how good my performance was at the company, I would never be seen as a worthy equal.

It was like all these microaggressions were being loaded into a sack on my back. Eventually they became so heavy that they weighed me down. And the prospect of new horizons became more attractive.

Meanwhile, there was the usual corporate politics and cliquishness that afflicts most white-collar environments, though on Wall Street the backbiting is amplified. This wasn't the case at the beginning, when there were only five of us in the office. Then it was great. But by the time I left a few years later, there were one hundred people there. This rapid growth was obviously a sign that business was thriving, but it took something away from the collegial, we're-building-something-together spirit with which we started.

There was one guy in particular who caused me vexation: Luke Haran, CEO of Serfin New York. He was an American whom the parent company hired out of Merrill Lynch to run the firm. And what he wanted was to remake Serfin New York as another investment bank. He regarded retail investing, which was my bread and butter, as inferior. (This is not an uncommon attitude on Wall Street.)

"In one underwriting, we can make a million dollars. Why are we bothering with making a hundred bucks from retail clients?" he said.

"Well," I said, "$100 multiplied by two thousand trades is $2 million. There's money in retail."

After a lot of this kind of thing, I grew so frustrated that I quit. There was a revolt in Mexico among the advisors, who backed me, as I was making the firm lots of money selling various products. Luke and I spoke, and we agreed on my return, but by then there was no turning back. My time in New York was drawing to a close. It was time to look for the next thing.

Luke was not a bad guy, but we had a different vision. In any event he was still the boss, and I was acting like a cowboy. And what have cowboys always done when opportunity dries up? They look to the West, where the open plain unfurls to the wide horizon and the setting sun …

New Frontiers: San Antonio

Although Federico didn't stick around New York for very long, he still had big plans for the company.

When he returned to Mexico, he championed an initiative to establish satellite branches in other American cities closer to our head-quarters. Eventually, the plan came to fruition.

"When you open the first office, I want that one!" I told Federico. I was ready for a change and excited to lead a new office essentially by myself. Starting over again and building something from the ground up.

And that was how I came to head Serfin's office in San Antonio, Texas.

I left New York in January 1994 to set it up. It was primarily focused on serving the Mexican high-net-worth client base we had served in New York but on a more personal basis.

Meanwhile, I had to learn new skills involved in managing a branch: negotiating a lease, hiring staff, marketing.

Things were going well that first year, but by Christmas of 1994, Mexico's currency crisis had knocked the whole country flat on its back and us with it. What happened was that the Mexican govern-ment devalued the peso, spiking interest rates and sending inflation skyward, which caused a ripple effect throughout not just the economy of Mexico but other economies of Latin America and Asia. It got so bad that Bill Clinton had to effectively bail out the Mexican government by lending $20 billion in a controversial aid package. (Mexico paid back the loan three years ahead of schedule.)

In the midst of this crisis, everything was turned upside down, and we had to change tacks. As it turned out, the sudden volatility of the peso, which had been stable for so long, presented opportunities for foreign exchange.

I made a deal with a bank to change our office to a foreign exchange operation. I started traveling from one end of the border to the other, from San Diego, California, to Brownsville, Texas, dealing with import-export companies that needed to either buy or sell dollars. While Serfin as a whole was barely treading water, my office was doing quite well.

That's why it came as a shock when the company told us they were going to shut us down. By then the government had taken over the bank, and they didn't want to pay salaries in dollars to Mexican citizens living in the States. Politically it looked bad, even though we were effectively contributing to the bottom line—paying for our own salaries and then some.

The higher-ups at Serfin offered to keep me on if I was willing to relocate back to Mexico. I also received job offers from Merrill Lynch and J. P. Morgan. These were prestigious, well-compensated jobs. But they didn't resonate with what I *really* wanted to do, which was to have my own firm, something created in my own vision, with my own team. The classic entrepreneurial dream that has always motivated dreamers and doers.

My time in New York and San Antonio had taught me a lot of valuable things. One was that fortune favors the bold. Throw your hat in the ring even if the odds are against you. Don't take no for an answer; don't be discouraged by initial rejection. Sometimes you have to plow through a hundred nos before you get a yes.

I also learned the value of nonconformity. If you do the same thing as everyone else, you will merely fade into the background. If you want to get noticed among the crowd, you've got to be different.

The corporate world tends to be myopic and set in its ways: things tend to be done merely by habit and routine,

Fortune favors the bold.

not because it's the best way That provides opportunities for innovators who buck the trend. Think about novel ways of doing routine tasks. Break from business as usual. Try something new or even radical.

When you question the status quo, you discover ways of improving that no one else has seen. That's how you get to the top.

Wall Street also taught me that I would likely always be perceived as an "other" and that in order for me to join the club, I couldn't just stand out in the rain knocking on the door until someone let me in. I'd have to build my own door. I'd have to build the whole damn house.

It was time to go into business for myself.

CHAPTER 4

ONE STEP CLOSER: SAN DIEGO

In 2009, the house where I grew up caught fire. Luckily my grandfather escaped, but the abode was rendered uninhabitable. We moved my grandfather to a new place and left the partially destroyed house standing there.

From time to time, my mother would go back to check on things or retrieve items we had left there. One day, she found among the ruins a letter I had written to her and my grandmother when I was twenty-two. I was living in New York at the time, and in the letter I had announced my decision to stay there following the IBM internship.

"It's hard here, but it's a great opportunity, because one day, it will lead to me owning my own broker-dealer," I wrote.

I had completely forgotten writing that letter, but it reminded me of the fact that I had long had my sights set on heading a company. I wasn't there yet, but with my next move, I took a great leap forward.

When I left Serfin, I couldn't just wave a wand and create a broker-dealer out of thin air. I lacked the resources, and even with my abundance of audacious self-confidence, I knew I didn't yet have the necessary experience for such a venture.

At the same time, I didn't want to move to another corporate job with a big bank and be a cog in the wheel for a few more years.

Instead, I found a happy medium as an independent broker affiliated with Investment Placement Group (IPG), a broker-dealer.[1] And that's how the next chapter of my life took me to the sunny shores of San Diego.

In order for a broker to operate, he or she must be affiliated with a broker-dealer, which must subscribe to an array of licensing requirements. This makes it attractive for independent brokers to operate under the aegis of a larger organization. It's a little like being a franchisee of a restaurant chain (with one difference being that the broker can create his own brand).

Eventually, I knew I would helm my own broker-dealer. But in the meantime, IPG would provide the entrepreneurial freedom of running my own company with the resources and legal framework of being attached to a larger operation. A kind of hybrid approach.

With this arrangement, I was losing the security of a guaranteed paycheck, since 100 percent of my salary would come from commissions. That meant a very low floor—but also a very high ceiling. It was up to me to make the most of it.

As before, I was eager to see what I could do on my own when faced with a new challenge and new environment. I wanted to put myself to the test.

I christened my brokerage as Precise Investment Management. Then I got to work.

---

1   A broker-dealer buys and sells securities for clients but also engages in trading for itself.

Arriving in San Diego

San Antonio, for all its charms, did not really suit me. I had missed the manic energy and buzz of New York City, and while San Diego is not nearly as frenetic as New York, I found it was more my speed. Its perennially fantastic weather let me indulge my affinity for outdoor sports. And I loved living near the ocean. All in all, it was an easy transition from the Texas plains to the Southern California coast. IPG's San Diego office was small and fraternal. There were a few partners, a few other independent guys like me, a little trading room—that was it.

Each time I opened a new account, it was exciting. And my early success helped address my own insecurities at the time. When you're a broker working for a big firm and you land a new client, you always wonder who the client is really signing on with: you, or the company you work for and its prestigious brand. But the steady growth of my own client list reassured me that I knew what I was doing, that I was good and could hold my own against larger competitors.

For the first few months, my income was a mere fifth of what I had been earning at Serfin. It was truly "eat what you kill." But eventually I clawed back and started earning even more than I had in New York, which validated that I had made the right decision.

A Day in the Life

I'm a morning person, which is fortunate because the markets in New York opened at 9:30, so I'd have to be in the office in downtown La Jolla around 5:30 a.m.

I'd have one list of clients and one list of prospects. First I'd handle client responsibilities, then start working on prospects. Being on the hunt got my juices flowing—ignited the hunter's instinct in me.

Every trade completed and deal closed and client signed elicited an adrenaline rush. I had done well in sales before, but when it's your own enterprise, the thrill is greater.

By the time the closing bell rang on the East Coast, it was only 1:00 p.m. in California, so I had the rest of the day to enjoy.

In the warmer months, I'd leave work and walk to the sea and swim among the sea lions, which to this day is one of my favorite things to do in San Diego. Many evenings I'd spend playing rugby in an adult rec league or hanging out with my teammates, who became my San Diego family.

The next day, I'd be back at work, 5:30 sharp, in front of my Bloomberg terminal. On the hunt.

My clients were primarily high-net-worth individuals in Mexico and institutions that cater to high-net-worth Mexicans. And this group of investors is attracted to different asset classes than the average retail investor. Their goal is usually capital preservation, since they've already made their money; they just want to keep it. They don't need to risk their money on more volatile assets.

When people talk about "the market," certain asset classes get most of the attention. The stock market, the S&P 500, IPOs, etc. But all that is just the tip of the iceberg. The real money, the big markets, are the bond market, debt obligations, borrowing from banks, insurance companies, governments, etc. And that's what I was trading. Bonds also have much higher minimum investments than equities, usually $100,000 to $200,000, so if you want a diversified portfolio in bonds you need at least half a million. In those days, bond ETFs didn't really exist, so it was a rather exclusive area.

And there's a *lot* of money to be made there.

I continued to specialize in the Mexican market, and the Mexican economy was still reeling from the fallout of the crisis that tanked Serfin. There were a lot of companies in distress, but once again, wherever there is distress, there is also opportunity.

I figured out how to capitalize on the situation and started marketing myself as a distress expert. When a company borrows money through the bond market, the investor is lending money to the issuer. If the company is unable to pay back the obligation, the debt needs to be renegotiated, sometimes in bankruptcy court, sometimes outside the courts. In Latin America, bankruptcy courts are, to put it mildly, inadequate and inefficient, so when the issuer got in trouble, there wasn't much of an established mechanism to protect investors' rights.

> Wherever there is distress, there is also opportunity.

I served as a go-between, negotiating between my clients and the bond issuers that were in trouble and working out a solution. In time it became my specialty, as my clients would purposely buy debt after it became troubled at pennies on the dollar and leverage my skills to negotiate something that would deliver an even greater return. I became, in effect, a "vulture investor"—and for this service, I was in high demand.

In a short time, I became IPG San Diego's biggest earner. I was even taking business away from major players like Morgan Stanley. I wasn't afraid of going up against the goliaths of Wall Street.

I remember one such incident fondly. One of my clients was a small Texas bank called Mercantile Bank, which was owned by a wealthy family in Mexico. In 1998 the family sold the bank to Wells Fargo for around a quarter of a billion dollars in stock, issued in physical certificates.

I was going to lose the bank as a client once Wells Fargo took over, but I thought I could at least keep the *family* with my book of business. They were about to get a $250 million windfall, and it had to end up somewhere.

I had a good relationship with the bank president, Graciela Gutierrez, who put in a good word for me with the family.

But there were sharks in the water, and they smelled blood. Everyone was doing their dog and pony show to woo the family: Morgan Stanley, J. P. Morgan, a few other big names. Eventually, the family narrowed the list to two prospects: a guy in Miami working for Merrill Lynch and me.

I needed to find an angle to outmaneuver Merrill Lynch—a real David vs. Goliath showdown if there was one.

I considered the angles I could play, then got Graciela on the phone. I knew that once you get custody of the account, it's harder for someone to take it away. That was the crux of my strategy.

"You've got the certificates in the office in Brownsville. If the office catches fire, those certificates can be destroyed," I said.

"They're registered," she said. "They can be replaced."

"Yes, but at a cost of 1 percent. That's 2.5 million bucks just to reissue them. But if you put them with me and Bear Stearns, there's no risk." (Bear Stearns was my clearing firm at the time.)

She realized I was right. So what did she do? Told her secretary to call Merrill Lynch and ask when someone could pick up the certificates.

Shit! I thought. *That was not the plan!* They were about to take my idea and let the other guy run with it, leaving me out in the cold.

But then they were told they would need a Brinks armored truck, and there was no route going through Brownsville. It would have to be a kind of special delivery that would take a few days to arrange.

I saw my opening.

"I can do it tomorrow," I offered.

She conferred with the family and agreed. I hung up the phone, bought a plane ticket from San Diego to Dallas, then caught a flight from Dallas to Harlingen, Texas. The president of the bank was waiting for me at the gate with the certificates.

Then I turned around and got back on the same flight, which was returning to Dallas. The elderly lady next to me struck up conversation. "Here on business?" she asked.

"Oh, just running a little errand," I said. Little did she know I had $250 million in stock under my seat.

When the plane touched down, I drove straight to Bear Stearns's office and deposited the certificates. And the family remains a client of mine to this day.

No Such Thing as Free Parking

For several years I was very happy with my work and with my life, relishing the laid-back Southern California lifestyle and making great money for someone of my age.

However, as the Buddha teaches, we are never satisfied. We are imprisoned by a yearning for more—for better or worse.

I still had a dream of owning my own business. It wasn't just money I wanted but the lure of building something big from scratch.

And also, that insatiable desire for novelty, for a fresh challenge. To leap over the canal and see what else is out there, in the fields beyond the fields.

So things were going well, but I didn't want to stay a broker forever. An opportunity presented itself when Leon Kassel, one of the three partners, announced his retirement.

I approached the other two with an offer to buy out Leon's share and replace him as the third partner. This seemed to catch them by surprise. They said they'd discuss it and let me know.

A week went by with no word. I followed up. "We're still thinking about it," they told me.

It seemed they were stonewalling. I went back a third time and said, "Are we going to do this or what?"

"Sorry, Carlos. We decided against it."

"You could have told me," I said. "You'd think you'd want to keep your biggest producer happy."

They offered to bump up my commission from 50 to 55 percent—plus a parking spot. A counteroffer that felt more like an insult than a good faith effort to keep me on.

At that moment, the writing was on the wall: I didn't have a future at IPG.

I looked around for opportunities at other broker-dealers, and I ended up signing with Chicago-based Horwitz & Associates in 2002 as an independent registered representative and advisor.

Quietly, I arranged to make the transition. One advantage of Horwitz was that they used the same clearinghouse as IPG. First,

I needed to reach out in confidence to Bear Stearns to adjust some conditions to complete the transfer. But for some reason, someone at Bear Stearns tipped off IPG's partners.

One afternoon, I came back from lunch, and the partners called me into their office and said, "We just found out you are leaving us, and we want to know why."

"I asked to make partner, and you rejected me. That's fine. I accept it. But I need to move on."

"You can't take our clients with you."

"They're my clients, actually. I found them. I put in the work. They belong to me." In truth many of my clients were people and firms I had cultivated since the Serfin days. So it was audacious for them to insist that.

"Well, then you're fired."

It was a classic "You can't fire me—I quit!" moment. I had already signed with Horwitz. Granted, this latest development kind of expedited my departure prematurely, but clearly, it was time to go.

They sent me a letter that formally announced my termination, then another letter that demanded a noncompete agreement, which I refused to sign. It was another audacious attempt to preemptively cripple my business, whether out of spite or some other motive. But I was under no legal or ethical obligation to put my name on the dotted line.

Naturally, they were irked at my refusal. Things were deteriorating rapidly, and I knew time was of the essence. The next move would be to lock me out of my own computer. In an abundance of caution, I uploaded all my client contacts and account numbers to a flash drive, walked out, and hit the beach.

That was the last day, for all intents and purposes, that I worked at IPG. The next morning, as expected, I found that my passwords had been changed and I couldn't get into my accounts.

Despite this acrimonious end, I look back fondly on my time there, and I learned a lot. The experience boosted my self-confidence. Although I was affiliated with IPG, I basically had to build my own brand from the ground up.

I learned that above all, what counts is *relationships*. Even more than performance.

And I learned that people can and will lie to your face. They'll break agreements and go back on their word. I learned how to be cautious without becoming cynical. To build up armor without losing your faith in humanity and your enthusiasm for the work.

This lesson, I would come to realize a few years later, would be the most important of all.

CHAPTER 5

THE BIG GAMBLE

I ended up working for ten years in San Diego for Horwitz, inching toward my dream of owning my own business. I was in communication with Horwitz's home office in Chicago every day, but for the most part they stayed out of our hair.

The first five years, from 2002 through 2007, things proceeded apace, with constant growth, until the Great Recession of 2008–2009 turned the whole financial world on its head. No one who worked in the financial services industry was unaffected. Suddenly our clearing firm, Bear Stearns, was in major distress and had to be acquired in a forced marriage by J. P. Morgan. Venerable firms like Lehman Brothers were gone; others teetered on the edge of bankruptcy. Our clients' portfolios were devastated, and even the safe investments were impacted. There was no refuge. That was my first business existential crisis, and I was truly scared, like most of us on Wall Street. If you lived through that time, you probably remember it well: for a brief but harrowing period, it seemed like the global financial system was about to collapse.

Typically, periods of upheaval lead to a lot of litigation. One client who did not heed my advice to sell after Fannie Mae got taken over by the government filed an arbitration, FINRA's version of a lawsuit, against me. The process was miserable, but it prepared me for things to come. The arbitration panel, which takes the place of the judge and jury, denied all claims, and it turned out that the client had an unlicensed advisor in Australia who was telling her not to listen to me. (When the market tanked, he committed himself to a mental institution.)

Resolving that took me three years, but I was ultimately cleared of all wrongdoing in March 2012. That was a momentous year for me. In May of that year I got lost in the desert. And in December, I made the move to buy Horwitz, fulfilling my dream of owning my own broker-dealer. I officially closed the purchase on December 20, 2012—the best Christmas gift I've ever given myself.

Coincidentally, as I was packing my things in San Diego in preparation for the relocation to Chicago, Federico, my old professor and colleague, was in town on business and rang me up. We hadn't spoken in years, but his timing was fortuitous. We arranged to have dinner together, where I told him the big news. "I'm proud of you, Carlos," he said. "Of all my students, I always thought you had the biggest potential."

Of course, he had essentially given me my start in the industry, so this chance meeting felt very significant, ceremonial even. Like cracking a bottle of champagne on the bow of a newly commissioned ship.

And then, it was time to get to work.

In truth, not a whole lot changed after the transfer of ownership, especially since I retained the firm's chief operating officer, Jerry Schwartz, who was the one who recruited me in 2002; in fact he liked to quip, "I recruited Carlos, and I now work for him!" I had been working with Horwitz for a long time so the staff already knew me. I called everyone into the conference room my first day and said, "I have something important to ask and I want the decision to be yours. What do you want the dress code to be?"

It was a lighthearted question (though in truth no matter is more serious in the office than whether and when you can wear jeans), but I wanted to set a precedent: that I wasn't interested in being a unilateral, top-down manager. I wanted the employees to have a stake in making decisions that affected all of us. After a vigorous debate, collared shirts and jeans (no ripped allowed) won the day.

Other than that, the only significant change I made was to the name: InSight Securities. I came up with the new moniker during a meeting with my attorney in Houston. We thought it was unlikely that such a name wouldn't have been taken, since the concept of "insight" is so central to finance and business, but by some miracle, it was there for the taking.

And thus the new firm was born.

Charting a New Course— and Rough Waters Ahead

Another early alteration I made was lowering the cubicle walls to open up the office space. Emotionally it was very rewarding to see the buzz of activity on the floor—to see my staff laughing and interacting with one another while working hard.

I also developed a proper trade desk, which the firm had lacked. My background was in trading, so it seemed prudent to bring this specialized knowledge to the company. I interviewed and hired two amazing women, Trish Coutre and Erika Badillo, who didn't have a lot of trading experience but were willing and able to learn. I mentored them and showed them the ropes, and their skills developed. In many ways the trade desk became the heart of the operation.

I had to focus my attention across different departments since I needed more robust staff. The Horwitzes hadn't really invested in personnel, or at least not the way I sought. As I brought new people on board, past experience wasn't priority number one; in fact some of my hires had little to no experience. I preferred to recruit people who were a blank slate. I needed fresh blood, someone I could teach, who had no preconceptions. They say that when fresh army recruits head to boot camp, the best marksmen end up being not the farm boys who grew up shooting and hunting but the ones who never handled a rifle in their life. That's because it's easier to train an eager novice how to shoot properly than to make an experienced guy who never learned the right technique unlearn a lifetime of bad habits. It was the same principle here.

The first months, however, weren't all smooth sailing. Within six weeks after receiving FINRA approval for the acquisition, in May 2013, I received a letter from FINRA's "anti–money laundering task force" announcing an audit. This came out of nowhere, like a bolt of lightning on the horizon.

Broker-dealers are routinely audited every two years by FINRA's local district office, and we had been audited recently. The agency had thoroughly scrutinized the company's books in order to approve the ownership transfer (which had officially been greenlighted a month before), and obviously, nothing had changed in the month since the approval to warrant such an intrusive inquiry. So what was going on?

It was the first skirmish in my long-running battle with FINRA.

This was anything but routine.

It was the first skirmish in my long-running battle with FINRA, which endures until this very day.

———

Jerry Seinfeld once joked that an IRS audit is for a taxpayer the financial equivalent of a complete rectal examination.

If that's true, then an AML FINRA audit for a broker-dealer owner is like having your kidneys surgically removed without anesthesia and passed around a room full of surgeons to examine, then asking you probing questions while you're waiting for them to stitch up your gaping wound.

Don't get me wrong; in our industry, auditing is par for the course, and generally, it is a good thing. It keeps everything and everyone above board and ensures there are no irregularities or improprieties. But when audits become aggressive, prosecutorial, or arbitrary, or when they are initiated for the wrong reasons, then it's a problem.

I talked to a friend who had been in the industry for a long time and had never seen anything like this. "You committed a major sin. A Mexican never buys out a Jew. In their eyes, you must be laundering money."

Fortunately, I had allies on my side. Jerry Schwartz, my COO, was one guy I could always count on. I called him my "Merlin": old, wise, sage, a valuable mentor, and a wizard of business and finance. He retired a couple years ago but still consults with me out of his house in Vegas.

"Not in my thirty years have I seen anything like this!" he said. And he had been dealing with the auditors from FINRA for a very long time.

According to Jerry, one problem with FINRA is that up-and-coming auditors try to prove their chops by being overzealous. It's how you make a name for yourself. Each auditor needs to find something. "You need to leave some kibble for the young dogs," said Jerry. A bone they'd have to take back to their bosses. It's like when you hear about aggressive, careerist prosecutors who look for a big, juicy red-meat case to get their name in the headlines. The problem is that this kind of attitude marginalizes the goal of pardoning the innocent and proving culpability for the guilty and turns the investigative apparatus of the state into a "game." "Winning" a big case that gets the DA headlines and a feather in their cap is more important than truth or justice.

FINRA is not a government body even though it has regulatory power, and therein lies another problem: because it is a private entity, there is no effective check on its authority. In my experience, the agency as a whole tends to be domineering and self-righteous. This quality would become especially apparent in the years to come.

I suspected someone had made a bad faith complaint to FINRA in an effort to bury me. It's not like I had any enemies, and I wasn't big enough to have any cutthroat competitors come after me, so who could it have been? My only thought was that it may have been Ed Horwitz, Gerald Horwitz's son, who thought himself the heir apparent to run the company after his dad retired and held a grudge against me as the new owner.

Ed, who was still working for the company after it became InSight, and I hadn't gotten along well. Originally he was going to stay on in the firm as an independent rep, but we had a falling-out. And he was tight with FINRA, being closely involved in licensing exams and whatnot. I wouldn't be surprised if he went to FINRA and said, "I have my suspicions about Legaspy, you should check him out." I am just speculating; I don't have any proof. But it's not beyond the realm of possibility.

In any effect, the genesis of the investigation didn't make any difference. I would have to face it regardless of its source.

So, FINRA descended on us with a platoon of auditors spitting out harsh questions like gunfire and tearing through our records with the fury of an invading army. For about eighteen months, they had four or five people in our office every day. For a firm of our size, an audit of this nature is severely disruptive. It drew a lot of my staff away from their responsibilities in order to deal with the auditors' requests.

It took so long that the inquiry was still in progress by the time we were due for the *next* routine audit, so for a while I had two different teams of FINRA auditors circling me like buzzards: the AML team and the regular district audit!

I remember one guy out of the Philly office; let's call him Frank. He was kind of our antagonist. He had been lingering in our Chicago office a while. One Friday afternoon, I asked, "So will we see you on Monday?"

"No. Someone else will be here," he said.

"Where are you guys going?" I asked. He was elusive in his response.

Jerry and I surmised that the AML team was planning to descend on one of our branch offices. We didn't want our independent reps handling the auditors—they weren't trained in how to deal with that situation, and it was really a heavy burden to ask them to shoulder. It would be a paperwork massacre.

Jerry and I put our heads together and tried to anticipate FINRA's next move, like a general and a lieutenant tracking enemy troop movements on a map. We figured Frank and his team were either going to our Miami office or the one in San Diego, where we had our two biggest operations, after the HQ in Chicago.

"Let's go!" I said. We were going to head them off.

Jerry hopped on a plane to San Diego, and I flew to Miami. When we landed, each of us waited for a call from the respective branch offices.

I sat calmly in my hotel room, waiting for the phone to ring. Finally, our receptionist Maria Elena dialed me and said, "There's a FINRA guy here. What should I do?"

"Stick him in the conference room," I said. "I'll be there in five minutes."

You should have seen their faces when they saw me walk into the office. "Hey, you guys are in Miami too?" I said. "What a coincidence! I was just dropping by for a visit. I'm happy to work with you here."

The same scene repeated in San Diego: Jerry was lying in wait at the receptionist desk in the office when in walked the auditor. "Good morning, gentlemen. What can I do for you?" he said with a knowing smirk.

But where was Frank? We found out later that day. In the afternoon I got a call from Ricardo in San Antonio, where Frank had showed up and helped himself to the files.

Still, at least we got two out of three.

FINRA has a mission, but just because they are, in theory, there to uphold norms, laws, and standards of the profession does not mean that they are not capable of overreach or abuse of power. If you're a broker or business owner, you've got to protect yourself from such overreach.

I tried to maintain a positive spirit through this protracted and totally unnecessary audit, but I was angry. I felt violated. It felt like there was an agenda; it wasn't just "fact-finding." I felt like they had made up their minds I was guilty and were going to keep digging until they could get me on a technicality or something. I'm not saying FINRA did that, but as the months wore on with no end in sight, that sickening feeling clung to me. It just didn't feel right.

What could I do but put my head down and try to conduct business as usual? I continued working hard to grow the firm. I hired new advisors and expanded beyond my Mexican clientele (which had been my bread and butter for years) to cast a wider net throughout the Western Hemisphere, including Central America, the Caribbean, Chile, and eventually an Argentinian group. Selling, as I said before, comes naturally to me.

When your business is clicking, growth becomes a virtuous cycle: more staff led to more business, which begat the hiring of more staff. I was running the firm on very thin margins. So I needed to aggressively grow revenues.

Our staff grew so much we eventually had to find new office space and moved to a new space in 2014. And that's when it finally, truly felt like my *own* firm and not one I merely acquired. I had to choose the space, design the layout—it was a symbolic break from the Horwitz legacy to the new Legaspy firm. By that point there were so many new people that the majority of the staff had no memory of the old firm.

It was a lot of fun despite the perpetual dark cloud of the audit.

At last, FINRA's AML report came out, and, except for a couple minor procedural errors on our part, we were cleared. There was no money laundering going on. The result also confirmed that in buying the firm, I had inherited strong procedures and protocol from Jerry, which put me at ease.

When FINRA finally left, I was so happy. And both audits (cycle and AML) were wrapped up around the same time.

We were in the clear, for now. But little did we know another storm was brewing. And if the audit was a tempest, the next crisis would prove to be a Category 5 hurricane.

CHAPTER 6

SOMETHING FISHY

Have you ever had a relationship that began in such romantic fashion, where you met by chance (or fate, as some might say)? And that person seemed so perfect at first, but you found out later they were just very skilled at concealing their many red flags? And finally, in the end, when everything went south, you rued the day that serendipity brought you together?

That's kind of how it was for me and Biscayne Capital, the company that became the bane of my existence and set in motion a chain of events that nearly destroyed my business and my career.

First, a brief explanation of the role of a broker-dealer and its relationship to clearing companies, account holders, and other parties. We (the broker-dealer) provide custody and execution agreement to a hypothetical Wealth Management Firm Inc.: their clients open accounts with us, which *they* (WMF Inc.) manage. We produce the account statements and execute the trades that they direct us to execute.

There are different kinds of broker-dealers. The old-school kind operates in a simple enough fashion: your broker advises you to buy AAPL, you agree, and the broker executes the transaction.

Then there is a service broker-dealer or institutional broker-dealer in which the client hires the financial advisor. So imagine your college buddy has a talent for stock picking or knows about personal finance and can devise a retirement plan for you. You hire him to create your personalized financial plan, but that plan has to be implemented, and he can't do it alone, so he engages an institutional broker-dealer (such as InSight, for example) that opens the account and processes the transactions.

Anyway, around 2014, in Latin America at the time, the clearing firms, which are the ones that provide the custody (the back-office services) for broker-dealers like mine, were consolidating. Some closed; others were bought out. And in 2014, J. P. Morgan closed the massive clearing operation they had inherited when they bought Bear Stearns in 2008.

When a clearing firm closes or exits the marketplace, it creates opportunity for other firms to snatch up the existing accounts, firms, and advisors who now need somewhere to go.

This trend created a big growth spurt for InSight because as a lot of accounts were "orphaned" by the wave of consolidations and closures, we captured a lot of business that needed a new home, and we placed it at Pershing, which was our clearing firm.

At the end of 2015, Raymond James also announced they were exiting the Latin American market, so every firm that cleared with Raymond James in the region needed to find a replacement. And that, too, created a great opportunity for us, given that we were focused on that market.

One company that reached out to us was Biscayne Capital, a

wealth management firm that primarily served high-net-worth individuals and families in Latin America. Biscayne had recently been sold to a new owner, and they were also clients of Raymond James; therefore, they were looking for a new place to place their accounts.

I didn't know much about Biscayne other than that they were a sizable operation, one of the biggest Latin American players. Given the change of ownership that occurred in 2016, the accounts were going to be managed by a new advisory firm called Total Advisors, which was going to be owned by Dario Epstein. Epstein was a prominent businessman with a strong industry reputation and was also well known for making occasional appearances as a commentator on CNN.

They were opening accounts in the hundreds. I was happy and proud that they expressed interest in working with me because larger competitors were also fighting for their business, but our pricing was more aggressive, so they ultimately chose InSight.

It was a challenging but enthralling period. Winning Biscayne's business was a boon for InSight. We were opening new accounts and transferring a litany of old ones to our control, around $700 million total.

During the time, I was introduced to two individuals who would play a pivotal role in the saga that was soon to unfold: one named Fernando Haberer and another named Gustavo Trujillo, who were responsible for running Biscayne's back office, which employed a couple dozen financial advisors.

Fernando was the sales manager, in charge of managing all the advisors. Fernando was in his early forties, of average height, fit, well dressed, and well groomed, with longish hair typical of the Argentinian upper crust, though he was a Uruguayan citizen of Jewish, Eastern European heritage. I really think if he had applied his talents for a good cause, he could solve world hunger. He was a brilliant, charismatic man—with, as I later found out, not one iota of morals.

Gustavo, who ran the back office, was in his midthirties. He was Ecuadorian with Amerindian features, and also very bright. He didn't have a college degree, but he had worked his way up in the industry and through the ranks of Biscayne. In many ways, sadly, he ended up being the fall guy for Biscayne's malfeasance.

I met with Epstein in Argentina, who kept me apprised of the situation with the company as its ownership changed hands and it moved to a new clearing firm. Everything seemed aboveboard.

Most of the $700 million coming into our custody were in the form of conventional assets: stocks, bonds, etc. But around November of 2016, I noticed we were holding a lot of securities in Biscayne's accounts that were unfamiliar: corporate bonds worth around $160 million issued by obscure companies I and I'm sure you have never heard of. Ocean Reef Corporation? Preferred Income Limited? What were these companies?

A quick note about how corporate bonds work, for readers unfamiliar with this aspect of finance. Companies raise money by issuing debt to investors. You give Company X $100 in return for a corporate bond backed by the promise that the issuing company will pay back the principal when the note matures, plus interest. Obviously, the healthier and more reputable the company, the more likely it is that you'll be paid back and your bond won't end up worthless. As the bond holder, you're more inclined to loan money to a company if you have faith they'll be around in a few years and will be able to service the interest and pay the principal on their debt. It's not necessarily improper when smaller companies issue debt, but it's something a custodian has to be aware of.

The bond market is *staggering* in its size—we're talking trillions of dollars in the United States alone, many times larger than the stock market. It is truly an engine of the economy, generating liquidity for companies of all shapes and sizes. Given the scope of the bond market, in one respect, $160 million is a drop in the bucket. In another, more pressing sense, for a relatively small firm like ours, that's enough debt to sink the ship if the notes end up being worthless.

I do a periodic review of the assets of our clients: what they're holding, asset allocation. It's not just due diligence; it's also fun and interesting for me. And it's a good way of detecting anomalies, like a radiologist studying an X-ray and noticing a suspicious lump. If you see it, you think, "What the hell is that? That's not normal."

And that lump was $160 million of bonds issued by those no-name companies.

When I probed more deeply, I discovered these securities had actually been issued by companies *owned* by the former owners of Biscayne—an obvious conflict of interest because it meant Biscayne had a financial incentive to get their clients to invest in securities that they (the owners) had a stake in. They had invested in real estate companies whose bonds they were advising their own clients to buy.

I asked my compliance department to look into it, and their research turned up a surprising development: a few years before, the SEC had undertaken its own investigation and also found that the former owners of the company had acted improperly by not divulging a clear conflict of interest, selling securities to their clients without proper disclosures that they were on both sides of the deal.

As part of the settlement agreement, the former owners of Biscayne had to divest themselves from the financial companies they owned to separate them from the issuers of those bonds. And that suggested to me that *that* was why they ended up selling to Epstein.

None of this had been known to me when Total Investment Advisers (formerly Biscayne, remember) inked a deal with InSight

Securities. These owners who were in charge while the SEC investigation was taking place had sold the company before I even came into the picture, and I had never dealt with any of them directly. But still, it left a bad taste in my mouth.

And regardless of what had happened already, the fact remained that now there was $160 million in privately placed securities that we were holding, and this made me uncomfortable. Even if those securities were legitimate, being priced, and making their scheduled interest payments, they were at best highly illiquid and thus hard to move.

At worst, they were a ticking time bomb.

Pershing Takes Notice

Have you ever turned into a dark alley late at night and immediately felt a sense of danger, but you also felt like it was too late to turn back? It was like that.

I felt like I was past a point of no return. And I wasn't the only one who had misgivings. Soon, Pershing, our clearing company, started asking questions about the dubious securities on the books. I don't know who or what tipped off Pershing, and they weren't especially forthcoming about things. They just told me: "We want them out."

When Pershing told me to get rid of them, I had no way of knowing if the notes were bad or not; I just wanted them off my balance sheet. I went back and forth with Pershing for a while as Pershing was pushing me hard to get rid of these accounts, even though the majority of the assets were normal securities. This put me in a difficult position, between a rock (Pershing) and a hard place (Total Advisors, to whom I was contractually obligated). Because you can't just make $160 million worth of your client's clients' assets "disappear." It's like if you're running an eldercare facility and one of the senior citizens stops paying rent. You can't just kick her to the curb.

Nevertheless, by September 2017, I had no choice but to tell Epstein and the others at Total, "Sorry, but Pershing is firm on this. You've got to take your business elsewhere." It was unfortunate because it was a significant source of revenue for the firm. But they had to go.

This process, however, was riddled with obstacles. When you're the custodian for a very large account that includes complex financial assets that are not easily liquidated or even transferred, it presents all sorts of logistical complications. It's not like where if the bank decides to cancel a retail customer's account, they just close out the checking account and cut the customer a check for the value of their savings.

Nor is it like the "old days," where securities existed in physical form and transferring ownership meant you could literally just stick them in an envelope and mail the stock certificates somewhere. Today, all those securities are in an electronic format called book entry form, which means that the only way that an account leaves a brokerage firm is because that customer opens a brokerage account somewhere else and moves the assets electronically.

Practically (and contractually) speaking, I couldn't really *force* Total out. I could only encourage them to sever ties and find a new custodian. I also needed to be mindful of not harming *Total's* clients (the ones who first held accounts at Biscayne, which then transferred those assets to InSight), as Total's clients were blameless in this whole mess. And because I was the custodian of their accounts, I had a commercial duty to fulfill.

So how does someone in my position gently compel Total to pack up and move out? A little bit of carrot and a little bit of stick.

It's like if you're a landlord and you want to evict a bad tenant pursuant to an eviction order, but there's no sheriff in town and thus no way to enforce the order. You can't physically remove him. You have to convince him to leave on his own by making things a little uncomfortable.

So I started "tightening the screws" by making it more difficult to conduct business, slow-walking requests, conditioning commission payments to a number of accounts leaving targets. One measure I took was to suspend any and all further purchase of these notes. I couldn't force divestment, but at least we wouldn't be buying more.

This was working. Little by little, we chipped away at the pile of bad securities, clearing out about half, leaving us with $80 million— better, but still a dangerous quantity of gunpowder to be carrying in the hull of your ship, where all it takes is an errant spark to ignite.

And I was still firmly ensconced between that rock and that hard place. By the waning months of 2017, Pershing was busting my nuts for not pushing out the risky accounts fast enough, while the guys at Total were dragging their feet because they couldn't find another custodian.

And then something truly ominous transpired: the companies that had issued the securities stopped making payments on their interest. Alarm bells were clanging.

Soon thereafter, worried calls started coming in from the clients of one of Total's advisors, Edith Hinojosa, whom I mentioned at the start of the book. Edith had a distinguished career working with Citibank and Bear Stearns. She was a shrewd salesperson who could, as the saying goes, sell ice to an Eskimo.

Her clients were complaining to me about not receiving interest on their assets. How interest works with securities is different from, say, an ordinary savings account held at a bank, and through my conversations with them it became evident that Edith had not explained to them certain things about the nature and risk of these assets (in other words, she had failed in her fiduciary duty to her clients). But there was also something odd about the calls—they all seemed kind of uniform, as if they were reading from a script. "You're my broker—it's your responsibility" was one repeated refrain and incidentally, not actually true—it *wasn't* my responsibility, but they were insistent. It was as if they had been coached to tailor their complaint a certain way.

That's when I found out that $50 million of the notes on our books had been sold by a single advisor: none other than Edith.

The unfortunate fact was that although we wanted to help them, there was nothing we could really do. We were merely custodians of their assets. Their calls should have been directed to Edith, but she had evidently disappeared and could not be reached, which naturally only intensified the anxiety of her panicked clients, who now feared they were holding a bag full of worthless bonds.

No one knew where Edith was, not even her colleagues at Total.

The calls from the clients continued through the end of 2017. Finally in December, I heard from the elusive Edith. We had never spoken directly before. Unsurprisingly, she played innocent.

"I'm being painted as the villain, but this isn't my fault!" she said.

"You were the one who sold those things to your clients," I said. "And now you're shirking your responsibility."

"Talk to Epstein," she countered. "We sold what we were asked to sell."

A classic case of passing the buck.

The Bomb Goes Off

In March 2018, we were still pushing accounts out—siphoning off the bad assets like frantically bailing out water from a sinking ship. But we had almost gotten all the assets out, and finally, the ship was righting itself. My back office was receiving hundreds of transfer requests, as

Total was steadily moving their clients' assets elsewhere, which made me happy.

Amid this deluge of requests, we were sent three letters of instructions for three of Fernando's clients requesting to transfer their accounts to Deutsche Bank. One of these accounts was held by one of the richest families in Argentina, a clan that had made a fortune from a Latin American media empire. (For discretion's sake, let's call them the Rossi family.)

Anyway, there seemed to be nothing out of the ordinary in these requests. Little did we know that these seemingly routine letters of instructions were concealing another act of fraud.

> Little did we know that these seemingly routine letters of instructions were concealing another act of fraud.

The transfers went through with no problem, but in May 2018, we got a call from the independent trustee that manages one of those accounts that was transferred to Deutsche Bank in March to ask us if we could reset their password to log into the account. In and of itself, that isn't unusual; people lose their password.

The InSight advisor who took the call noticed the communication from the trustee had a string of emails that included Fernando as a recipient, something to the effect of "Dear Fernando, please find this statement attached …" And then Fernando forwarded it to the trustee.

The email chain *appeared* to include a statement sent by my advisor. But the advisor, upon seeing this, told me, "I never sent this original email."

By all appearances, it certainly looked like he did. It contained a perfect facsimile of one of our statements—but it was fake. A forgery. In other words, that email was fabricated to give the appearance that the fake statement originated with my employee. It was a remarkably simple but effective ploy: the email would say, "Fernando, here's the requested statement" and then Fernando would "forward" it to the trustee, who would naturally think it originally came from our advisor.

I had to go into the server to confirm my advisor's claim that no such email was sent. Moreover, as we scrutinized the email chain more closely, we saw that it included a PDF that contained a falsified monthly statement from that account but was not showing the over $6 million that had been transferred in March. It's really not that hard to cook up a fake PDF statement. You could probably do it in Word or Microsoft Paint in ten minutes. And this fake statement showed the account had $6 million in assets, but we confirmed that it actually had $100,000. The rest had been transferred to Deutsche Bank.

It was a puzzling discrepancy. One question begat another.

I called the client—the owner of the account whose numbers were being fudged—who was unaware of any of this.

Then I confronted Fernando in search of answers, and he said this was just a misunderstanding, it was transitory, told me not to worry. Well, obviously a fake email and forged account statement is not caused by a "misunderstanding," but it didn't necessarily mean Fernando was the guilty party. It didn't exactly absolve him either, though. Was he the perpetrator or just an unwitting victim?

The more twisted the case became, the more I was determined to find the truth.

Basically, what had happened was that Fernando was managing money with us, as well as with clients at Deutsche Bank. As you know, we had imposed restrictions on purchasing Biscayne notes, but Deutsche Bank had not placed such a restriction. So any time Fernando needed liquidity, he'd sell more notes to his clients whose accounts were held at Deutsche Bank.

In other words, once InSight suspended using Total's clients' funds to buy the worthless notes, Fernando had to find another pool of capital to do so (earning commission from each purchase). And then when there was no more cash available in the Deutsche Bank accounts, he started *overdrafting* those accounts.

So by March 2018 the account was overdrafted by $12 million as a result of Fernando's machinations, and he had stuck the Rossis with $50 million of worthless notes.

Suddenly Deutsche Bank wakes up and busts Fernando's balls. As shown in records that we later subpoenaed, Fernando told Deutsche Bank he would cover the overdrafted balance. Fernando showed them a client statement—with no account holder name—from J. P. Morgan supposedly showing "assets under [Fernando's] control," which Fernando said would be transferred to pay down the overdraft.

Deutsche Bank clearly didn't care whose money would cover the money owed to them, so long as it got covered.

However, the account at Deutsche Bank he was controlling belonged to a different customer than the accounts he was managing with us (there were literally different names on the accounts). So Fernando needed to figure out how to get the assets from the customers with us to the Rossis' overdrafted account. His scheme was to take those securities that were intended for the specified clients that we sent and put them into the overdraft account, sell the securities, and pay down the overdraft. He orchestrated this scheme through the absurdly simple method of falsifying the PDF to change account names and numbers, to make it look like account A (held at InSight) belonged to the same party as account B (held at Deutsche Bank).

Transferring securities is really no different than mailing a check: the address on the envelope indicates where the check should go, and if the recipient does not live at that address, or the address doesn't exist, it gets returned to sender. However, the forged instructions only got the assets to Deutsche Bank's door. Fernando needed to get the securities to the overdrafted account, which was different from the instructions (address) that we sent. To this very day, I don't know how he did it, but I suspect he had an accomplice on the inside who would disregard our instructions, not return the securities to sender because the accounts did not exist, and post them into the account that owed money to Deutsche Bank.

Basically, he was using the Rossis' own money to pay the overdraft, like moving money from your left pocket to your right pocket. The problem was that the right pocket had a big hole in it. He was stealing from one of Rossi's companies, and his relatives, to pay another person's debt. Robbing Peter to pay Paul.

At this point, Fernando and I were still in contact, but he was, to put it generously, less than forthcoming about what was happening. All I could say to him was "You made your bed, so lie in it." This was a mess of his own making. And completely criminal.

I also spoke to Gustavo, his associate. I actually liked Gustavo. Expecting major fallout from the scandal, Gustavo feared for his life and took his family to Miami, so I met with both the clients (whose money was stolen) and Gustavo.

Meanwhile I was still trying to figure out where the money went (I didn't know at the time which account it had ended up in). Fernando's robbed client was saying that there was no problem with his other account at Deutsche Bank, so why were their assets transferred there?

In the middle of this chaos, I decided that the only course of action I had was to file a criminal report to the FBI on Fernando with what I knew at the time.

Everything was falling apart quickly. And soon, I would be the one left to pick up the pieces.

The House of Cards Collapses

Charles Ponzi was not the originator of his eponymous scheme, but he did make it famous, having run a lucrative fraud that collapsed in 1920 and sent him to prison for many years on multiple charges. Bernie Madoff was the most recent huckster to become a household name for all the wrong reasons; his Ponzi reached into the tens of billions of dollars and defrauded thousands of investors, making it the largest such scheme in history.

Between Charles Ponzi and Bernie Madoff, there were many others, some famous, others forgotten, but the Ponzi remains an enduring weapon of choice among fiscal fraudsters.

Most people are familiar with the classic Ponzi, where you use the money from new investors to pay off old investors, often by inflating (i.e., lying about) the worth of the investments. It involves fake account statements. Total fabrications. The assets people are told they own are fiscal smoke and mirrors. It's a pyramid scheme, basically, that relies on misleading new investors about what they're actually buying. It can go on for a long time—Madoff ran his successfully for many years before it blew up in his face.

The classic Ponzi is actually not so easy to pull off these days (another reason why Madoff's malfeasance was so shocking). Today, with the separation of functions between custodians, advisors, and so forth, it's harder to fabricate statements.

Enter the *modern* Ponzi, which works as follows: securities are issued, so the investor owns a legit security, but *that* security, the company issuing it, is investing in the Ponzi. So the statement is real, the asset is real, but the security itself is worthless. If the schemers are able to fabricate the prices (the net asset value, or NAV), it's practically impossible to detect—until someone pulls out that card and the whole house of cards comes tumbling down.

That was what was happening before our eyes with Total Advisors.

In fact, the SEC had come very close to blowing the lid off the whole thing when they sanctioned Biscayne for conflict-of-interest violations. But the SEC failed to detect the Ponzi. The company managed to slip under the radar at that time, even as it was at the center of a Ponzi that had grown to hundreds of millions of dollars in assets by that point.

Once the schemers accumulated enough capital from investors, they used the "first generation" of those securities to develop real estate in Key Biscayne, a hot market that, like much of the real estate sector, imploded in 2008 when the global financial crisis hit. Biscayne might have filed for bankruptcy then (the fate of many other companies with overexposure to real estate), but instead, they exploited the captive, naive investor base they had developed and just kept issuing notes to pay off the old ones. They realized they had a money printer, as long as investors would buy the new notes, which paid the interest on the old ones, and the schemers kept the rest.

And so, the pyramid grew and grew. We estimate between $300 and $400 million of worthless securities were sold to investors across multiple firms in which the underlying asset was nothing but a Ponzi.

Biscayne used Deutsche Bank as an unwitting participant because Biscayne had an agreement with DB where they'd call DB and say, "Please reissue a million dollars of debt for this company." And DB would print a new promissory note and put it in Biscayne's account, and they'd sell that to investors.

Investors would own the security, and Biscayne would profit from the proceeds of the sale. The issuer deposits interest payments to the holders of the note, and when the note is due, they pay the principal. That's how it's supposed to work, anyway.

But as you know, these notes were backed by nothing. Biscayne just kept selling notes, paying the interest but with nothing in the coffers to back the principal. In this way they maintained the illusion.

A Ponzi needs new investors to keep going. When I imposed a restriction of no new purchases, I was unknowingly pulling out a card that was bearing the load of all the other cards stacked precariously on top of it. After that, the scheme dried up.

Biscayne needed liquidity to keep it going. They couldn't get it from new investors, so instead they'd essentially buy the notes on credit issued by DB. Their account at DB became overdrafted. They were borrowing from DB but couldn't pay it when they couldn't sell more notes.

Deutsche Bank, unsurprisingly, caught on to what was going on by the summer of 2017 and told them, in so many words, to pay the overdrafted balance and get the hell out.

But Fernando *could not* pay off the overdraft; he just moved it from one account at DB to another. That's when he used his access to the Rossis' account at InSight to pay off his debt to Deutsche Bank. Biscayne, to my knowledge, settled their outstanding balance with Deutsche Bank by transferring funds from the Rossis' account. Maybe they thought a family with such a high net worth wouldn't notice a few million missing.

So the Rossis got screwed on two fronts. And the worst was yet to come.

Lawsuits Pile Up

The whole debacle had resulted in a lot of people losing a lot of money as a result of some unscrupulous individuals. And they were angry. And what happens when people get angry? They sue.

I didn't know the full story about Edith at the time, but eventually I would learn that she was dogged by a trail of accusations and legal problems. She had been indicted in Ecuador (her native country) for other malfeasance. The courts compelled her to wear an ankle bracelet to prevent flight, but somehow she got it off, made her way out of Ecuador via a land border, and hightailed it to Orlando.

If you're an advisor, selling $50 million in bonds will net you a big fat commission. And she was living a lavish lifestyle as a result of this largesse.

But when things came tumbling down, she had to get her ass out of there. Some of her clients lost *all* their savings. So she said, "I'll help you recover by helping you sue this idiot in Chicago. Squeeze his nuts until he opens his wallet."

In July of 2018, I get served an arbitration from one of Edith's clients, to the tune of $1.5 million, in essence saying that, as the custodian, I should have known something was amiss and should never have allowed those securities to be purchased.

A month later, the Rossi family filed an arbitration, too, which named Pershing *and* InSight *and* me personally, accusing me of fraud—specifically, of colluding with Fernando to engineer the improper transfer of millions of dollars of assets to Deutsche Bank, which were essentially "lost." That arbitration was for $9 million.

I was reeling from this one-two punch when the next blow came in the form of a lawsuit from Edith's clients, who were represented by Akerman, a prominent Miami law firm. A friend of mine with his ear to the ground found out that Edith, who was the one who caused her clients' misery by selling them a boatload of worthless notes, was also the one rallying her bamboozled colleagues to participate in the suit. I obtained a copy of the engagement letter and the contract Akerman was distributing to the clients that included the provision that (paraphrasing) "you agree that Akerman cannot represent you in any suit against Edith Hinojosa." This disgusted one of the investors, who saw this as a clear attempt by Edith to save herself by shifting the blame onto me and my company. This investor was the one who sent me the engagement letter.

1. <u>Scope of Engagement.</u> You have retained us to represent you in a connection with the Potential Claims. **However, you understand that Akerman cannot represent you in any claims, actual or potential, adverse to Edith Hinojosa and/or Pershing, LLC.**

Anyway, what resulted from that were lawsuits in which 125 of Biscayne's were clients claiming damages of *$30 million.* (I was already missing the halcyon days when people were only suing me for a million and a half.)

The irony is that by questioning what had been going on, and plugging the purchase of fraudulent notes, I had jammed the gears of the whole charade. But now instead of being thanked, I was the one being targeted by multiple legal actions with the help of the perpetrators themselves.

And just when it seemed things couldn't get worse, in October 2018, Pershing told me they were going to terminate their clearing agreement with my firm, a kick in the ribs as I was already on the ground.

Just a few years into my stint as the owner of a broker-dealer, I was looking at the prospect of financial ruin. I knew I was innocent, but the financial, legal, and reputational damage the scandal was already causing was jeopardizing everything.

I thought back to my San Diego days, where I'd sometimes spot Ivan Boesky around town. Boesky, you may know, became notorious in the '80s for a giant insider trading scandal. Before the scandal broke, Boesky lived a high-flying, lavish life. Stories abound of his conspicuous consumption. For example, he would patronize fancy restaurants and order one of each entrée, taste each, and say, "I'll take this" and have the rest thrown into the garbage.

Boesky eventually pleaded guilty to insider trading and was fined $100 million—a fall as spectacular as his rise. After that, he was forced to live a modest life in San Diego, where I would occasionally see him in the food court with a plate of fried rice or driving a beat-up old Mercedes. I guess he wasn't doing so poorly; I mean, he seemed to be living a comfortable middle-class lifestyle. He wasn't destitute. But what a fall from grace. For him, it was probably painful to think about how he had lost so much and plunged so far.

I hadn't done anything wrong, but I couldn't help but think of Boesky and feel like Icarus a little bit. I had flown so high but had gotten too close to the sun. My wax wings were melting, just like in the myth, and I was in a freefall back to earth. Whether I'd land on my feet, or get smashed to pieces on impact, was anyone's guess.

CHAPTER 7
GUILTY UNTIL PROVEN INNOCENT

Rather than being rewarded for my vigilance, I was confronted with the biggest challenge of my life. The perpetrators, partly to shift blame away from themselves and partly to stick it to me for causing their scheme to collapse, had colluded with some of their clients to file six arbitrations (for an aggregate value of $40 million) against me and my firm.

Recall that, as FINRA members, we brokers are obligated to litigate any disputes with clients through arbitration within FINRA, in lieu of taking such disputes to court. And what's even worse, we can't file a counterclaim against anyone who is not a FINRA member, like Fernando or Edith. We just have to defend ourselves.

Now the problem with arbitration is that any accusation, regardless of what it's about or whether or not it has been heard, is immediately reflected on the broker being sued. It's like a billboard on the freeway for everybody to see. After an entire career spent building up goodwill and a reputable name, now the first thing that came up when you googled me was news of these arbitrations. So that throws presumption of innocence out the window. And then the whole cottage industry of ambulance-chasing attorneys piles on and runs ads saying, "If you were a customer of this corrupt broker, call us at 1-800-BROKER-FRAUD." This becomes a racket in which claimants' attorneys file arbitration against brokers, sully their names, and then extract some settlement in exchange for not pursuing the claim.

The accusations of fraud were maligning my name—and threatening the continued existence of my company—as I hurriedly tried to figure out what to do next.

Kangaroo Court

One of my favorite rugby traditions is something called "kangaroo court." It happens during the postmatch social (referred to as the "third half"). Here a member of one of the clubs dresses up as a judge, wig and all, and several players get put "on trial" for egregious offenses against rugby, like having hair product in one's kit, drinking with the wrong hand, or passing gas during a scrum.

Even though there is ostensibly a prosecutor and a defense attorney, the outcome is known ahead of time: "guilty!" and the player gets sentenced by the judge to drink beer out of his boot or stay at the bar wearing his underwear on the outside (provided the player was actually wearing underwear that day).

Of course, the term did not originate with rugby. A "kangaroo court" means a mock court where any claim to jurisprudence is phony or flimsy at best, and the usual norms and rules are ignored, discarded, or arbitrarily applied. Little did I know that I would be caught up in a "real-life" version of kangaroo court, with very serious potential consequences.

As I have explained before, FINRA is not a government agency, it is a not-for-profit corporation classified as a self-regulatory organization (SRO), and the SEC has deputized FINRA to regulate securities broker-dealers. There is a Depression-era law called the Maloney Act that mandates that all broker-dealers have to be members of an SRO. Originally there were several SROs, and broker-dealers could choose whom to affiliate with. However, in 2005 all SROs merged into a newly created FINRA. From that moment broker-dealers had no choice but to be FINRA members. And one of the conditions of FINRA membership is that you agree to handle disputes in arbitration.

One of the services that the National Association of Securities Dealers (NASD) offered was an extensive arbitration forum that they called dispute resolution service. FINRA inherited this service from NASD, and in it is now the largest securities dispute arbitration forum in the country. In 2020 there were 3,500 arbitrations heard, settled, or withdrawn.[2] The dispute resolution service is a big moneymaker. Both FINRA and the arbitrators get paid, and the fees are charged to the parties.

Arbitration is usually something that parties entering a contract agree to in advance, to avoid having to litigate in court. Those daytime court shows like *Judge Judy* or *The People's Court* are, despite having the appearance of a normal civil trial, nothing more than arbitration. The parties agree beforehand to have their cases decided by arbitrator Judy.

In real court there is something called Rule 11, which allows for sanctions against the attorneys for failing to perform a good-faith investigation on the merits of their client's claim. This is done to help prevent the filing of frivolous suits. Additionally, in court you can file a "motion to dismiss," which allows the defendant to request a preliminary review of the merits of the claim.

---

2   "Dispute Resolution Statistics," FINRA, accessed January 4, 2022, https://www.finra. org/arbitration-mediation/dispute-resolution-statistics.

In FINRA, however, anything goes. An attorney can make the most exaggerated and unsubstantiated claims, knowing that FINRA's BrokerCheck will display those allegations for the world to see and the defendant (or respondent, as he is called in arbitration) cannot request a dismissal. In one of the arbitrations I faced, we were being sued by clients who opened an account but never actually funded it. Consider the absurdity of arbitrators "needing to hear the merits" of a claim about an account that never had any money in it.

A couple of years ago I was driving down I-95 in Florida and saw a billboard that said, "Did you lose money in the stock market? Call 1-800-stockloss." Notice that it didn't say, "Did your broker do something wrong?" It implied, "You lost money in the market, probably due to unwise decisions on your part, but let's go after your broker anyway."

Because attorneys who represent claimants in FINRA know they can extract a hefty settlement, regardless of the merits of the case, they often go for the gangster approach: "Hey, broker-dealer, you got a nice firm there—it would be a shame if something were to happen to it ..."

I understand why you would want an alternative forum such as arbitration for smaller and straightforward claims, like "My broker told me to invest 100 percent of my savings into one stock," but complex cases give rise to a perversion of justice that deserves the moniker "kangaroo court." And not the fun rugby kind.

Pershing Pulls Out

For years, I had a great relationship with Pershing. But in the wake of all the litigation, things went south. I was on a business trip in Miami when I got a call from Pershing stating they were terminating the clearing contract and we had 180 days to transfer all assets out. I can only imagine it's akin to what it feels like when your doctor tells you that you have cancer: blindsided shock, followed by an insidious sense of dread. All I could think was, *What the hell can I do now?*

For a broker, the clearing firm is like the heart that pumps blood through the body of the business. The heart had stopped beating, and I needed a transplant fast. But it's not easy in the best of circumstances to get a new one overnight, and especially then, with all the controversy surrounding me.

I tried to maintain a facade of normalcy as I finished out the Miami trip even though inside I was shaking. I flew back to Chicago and spent the weekend in deep introspection, mulling my next move. What should I do? What were my options? Was there any way I could secure a new clearing contract?

One thing was certain: I wanted to keep this latest development with Pershing close to the vest. In time, if need be, I would inform my employees, but there was no reason to make them panic yet, and more importantly, if word got around that InSight was losing its clearing firm, it would make a bad situation worse.

The following Monday, a friend in Miami called me up. "Hey, Carlos, I heard your contract got terminated!" I hadn't told even my own managers, yet someone at Pershing had evidently leaked it. This would make my job even more difficult because now the cat was out of the bag. It would put me at a disadvantage in future negotiations with clearinghouses because they would know how desperate I was to find one.

I decided to try to do an asset sale, reasoning that I could recover the value of my investments if someone could buy my business—not the *firm*, since I still had legal liabilities, but the business, which technically speaking was a separate entity, something I could sell.

I reached out to a couple firms I was on good terms with, and they expressed some interest. We got as far as talking numbers and signing nondisclosure agreements, but news of the Pershing debacle and the tempest of litigation tanked the deal. The financial industry might seem vast and sprawling, but people-wise, it is really rather small, more like a gossipy village than a big, anonymous metropolis. And when scandal strikes, people talk. Once the firms I was negotiating with learned of my situation, they concluded, rationally, that there was no real reason to purchase any part of my business when they could simply wait around for the other shoe to drop. Since I was in a jam, they predicted that once my advisors would start heading for the exits, those firms could scoop them up (along with their book of business) without having to pay anything to InSight.

The Chicago winter is long, cold, and dark, and that winter was shaping up to be the longest, coldest, and darkest of my life. In January 2019, I get a nasty letter from an attorney named Martin Litwak stating that his firm was representing investors in the Biscayne notes and was contacting all of the custodians (such as InSight) that had clients who bought notes. The letter urged me to enter into settlement negotiations. Interestingly, Martin had been an attorney for the principals of Biscayne Capital, the ones who perpetrated the fraud in the first place. I thought, "Man, this guy has balls!" trying to play both sides.

The story got stranger after that. A friend of mine heard from a mutual acquaintance of his and Fernando's that if I paid $250,000 in cash, I could get out of the suit. It felt like a shakedown.

Needless to say, there were a lot of rumors and hearsay flying, in all directions, and I wanted to cut through the noise and have a man-to-man conversation. So I talked to Litwak directly. "Are you sure you wanna pick a fight?" I said.

"Let's talk," he said.

I agreed, but I wanted our phone conversation to be documented. I knew he wouldn't agree to be recorded, and I lived in

Illinois, where it's illegal to record another person on the phone without their consent. So the next best thing was to hire a court-certified stenographer in Puerto Rico who would be on the line during the phone conversation with Litwak. During my call with Litwak, which we conducted in Spanish (Litwak is originally from Argentina), he backed down while also denying the allegation about the $250,000 extortion. All of it was typed up and transcribed by the stenographer, surreptitiously listening in.

That was a small victory, but it only underscored my deepening crisis: everyone around me was trying to take a bite out of me.

Meanwhile, the clock kept ticking as I scrambled to find a new clearing firm. By April of 2019, about six months after Pershing first announced its impending termination, I wasn't any closer to a deal. The deadline was approaching rapidly.

> Everyone around me was trying to take a bite out of me.

Fortunately, I thrive when my back is against the wall. That's when I do my best work.

I pleaded with Pershing for an extension, and they agreed to give me another three months.

Then I racked my brain for a solution to the other problems, or at least some kind of temporary reprieve. It seemed that selling was out of the question. I was untouchable because of that metaphorical billboard above the highway that announced, "Carlos Legaspy is a fraudster!" (It may as well have been a real billboard!) However, I could still divest myself of the company while keeping it in the family: I could sell my business to my sister Myrna and finance it, and she could pay me in installments. Of course, she would still need a clearing contract to legally receive and operate InSight, but at least my name, which had been dragged through the mud, would not be attached.

Myrna agreed with the plan. Then, after many calls and frenzied negotiations, we worked out a deal with a clearinghouse called INTL FC Stone that offered Myrna a clearing contract. So by that summer, things were looking up again.

Our company's annual continuing education conference took place in Las Vegas in July 2019, when I announced to the advisors that I was selling the business to Myrna, while Stone would come in as the clearing firm to replace Pershing. Some advisors were shocked and said they would leave because they needed to continue working with Pershing, while others said they would leave because they wanted to work for me and not Myrna, whom they barely knew. But the majority expressed their intention to stay on.

So we lived to see another day …

———————

I told you earlier that rugby is a passion of mine, one of the highlights of my time in San Diego, which, looking back, was so comparatively carefree and pleasant.

One of the cool things about rugby, unlike, say, American football, is that if you're on the pitch, you play both defense and offense. And now it was time to apply some of the lessons of the sport that I loved to my current crisis: defending my territory while simultaneously striking back.

I did make some progress on one front. When Diego Rossi and his family filed the $9 million arbitration against InSight for processing the transfer instructions that Fernando gave us to transfer to Deutsche Bank for the benefit of the overdrafted account also owned by Rossi, it appeared that his attorney Jenice Malecki was in cahoots with Fernando. In the statement of claim, she included some private communications that I had with Fernando years ago. How did she get those communications? You do not need to be Sherlock Holmes to deduce that if *I* hadn't given those communications to her, the only other possible source was Fernando. This added that none of the clients were pursuing any claims against Fernando. I wasn't born yesterday, so I filed suit against Rossi, Epstein, *and* Fernando in the Northern District of Illinois, alleging conspiracy to commit fraud against me.

By July 2019, we reached a tentative settlement agreement with Rossi where he would get the limit of my insurance policy for $1 million, and we would mutually drop our suits against each other. That agreement was tendered through my insurance carrier, pending the carrier's approval. Which meant more waiting. The legal process truly is glacially slow, which can be agonizing when you have so much on the line. But sometimes all you can do is wait …

In the weeks following Labor Day 2019, two things happened. First, I resigned from my own firm and officially ceded control to my sister. Contending with all the litigation (dealing with paperwork, meeting with lawyers, etc.) had become a full-time job. I was overwhelmed and needed more time. Moreover, both the "outgoing" clearing firm (Pershing) and the "incoming" one (Stone) wanted me out of the business. My resignation felt humiliating, but I accepted it, knowing it was for the greater good, for myself, my family, my advisors, and the long-term health of InSight.

From here on out, I'd trust my management team to complete the deal and transfer assets from Pershing to Stone.

Everything was in place and moving. We were in the process of executing contracts, when suddenly, Stone reneged on their offer, stating they had changed their mind and no longer would offer a clearing contract to Myrna. And just like that, the rug was pulled out from under our feet again.

I don't know what accounted for their sudden reversal, though I suspect the motive was similar to why other firms had bailed on buying InSight's business: they saw we were a wounded animal and instead of expending energy to finish me off, they could just wait until I died an inevitable death; then they could pick off InSight's advisors directly.

I felt stabbed in the back and once again found myself in a desperate situation with no clearinghouse, no prospect for a deal, and Pershing refusing to extend the agreement once more, beyond September 19, 2019. The last grains of sand in the hourglass were falling away …

In a last-ditch, Hail Mary move, Myrna approached Pershing herself and asked for an agreement, since technically she was operating a new broker-dealer that was legally detached from me, and she argued that there was no reason Pershing couldn't establish a relationship with *her*, even if I was persona non grata. Pershing didn't shoot it down right away. They mulled it over for a few months, but by the end of the year, they declined her proposal.

Another hammer blow came at the start of the new year. In 2020, my insurance carrier denied coverage on the claims related to my settlement of the suit against Rossi, asserting that the dispute involved transfers, which were *not* covered by my insurance policy.

I really felt like my luck had run out.

The Loose Head Prop

Rugby, even more than most team sports, is a game of the unit rather than the solitary player. Everyone moves in tandem, a beefy, brawny brigade parading down the pitch.

Rugby also has some colorful-sounding positions. The "hooker" is, roughly speaking, the center of a wrecking ball called the scrum. His job is to "hook" the ball from the adversaries. The position requires coordination and decision-making. And each hooker is guarded by two "props" (loose head and tight head) in front, who protect the hooker as they go into the scrum.

If I was the hooker of the squad, my attorney Nicholas Iavarone was my prop. He was my legal muscle who supported me through all these arbitrations and lawsuits as we fought our way forward.

I love Nick. I started working with him when I bought the firm in 2012, and we've been to battle many times. He is a real character, an old-school, street-smart attorney who is in his seventies now and has a lifetime of experience under his belt. He used to be a prosecutor and was also the main litigator of Bear Stearns in Chicago.

He's got that pit bull toughness that you want your legal counselor to have, but he's lovable—a brilliant mind and shrewd strategist. He doesn't like being bullied any more than me. But when he questions a witness, he's impeccably polite and affable—in other words, he can be both fierce and aggressive, and gentle and disarming, depending on what the situation calls for. He's taught me a lot.

I was feeling overwhelmed, but with Nick on my side, I knew I had an ally.

And so, in 2020, the myriad legal battles continued. Hours and hours of discovery requests, obtaining documents, handling inter-rogatories. An exhausting, draining, gargantuan task.

The next frustration involved another engagement with Akerman. A little background: In order for the Biscayne scheme to work, when the SEC sanctioned Biscayne, the culpable individuals legally divested their interests and placed them in an irrevocable trust called Vanguardia. The trustee was a company called Amicorp. Diego Rossi filed suit in Florida against the Biscayne players along with Amicorp, which at that moment was the legal owner of the fraudulent note issuers (held in the aforementioned trust).

Guess which firm appeared to represent Amicorp? Akerman! That suggested to me Akerman was buttering both sides of the bread—representing Edith's clients and at the same time representing the owners of the issuers of those fraudulent notes, in a different case.

If this had played out in court rather than FINRA, it would have been automatic disqualification due to conflict of interest. But because it was being litigated in FINRA, I had no option but to sue Akerman in Florida civil court, seeking disqualification based on Akerman's conflict of interest. If I were to succeed in that suit, Akerman would be disqualified in their suit against *InSight*, thus taking care of that $30 million claim hanging over my head. It was part of my strategy of defending myself by counterpunching my adversaries.

I also filed a third-party claim within the arbitration against Deutsche Bank Securities because Deutsche Bank Securities were the ones who sold the stolen securities that were transferred to Deutsche Bank. There's a FINRA rule that says any dispute between member firms must be decided within FINRA arbitration. You can't try to enjoin a fellow member to refrain from arbitrating against you.

Well, Deutsche Bank ignored that rule and turned around and sued me in New York. I went to FINRA and said, "Hey, I just got sued by a fellow member in violation of your own organization's rule." But FINRA did nothing. If the roles had been reversed, and I had sued a member to prevent a fellow member from arbitrating against me, I'm sure they would have rained hellfire against me.

I can only surmise that FINRA declined to enforce the rule because the violator in this case was a big firm. (When it comes to financial institutions, it doesn't get much bigger than Deutsche Bank.) I guess FINRA enforcement attorneys might want to work one day for Deutsche Bank.

So I had to defend myself in New York court against Deutsche Bank's suit while fighting an arbitration involving Deutsche Bank—another front opened in an ever-expanding and increasingly acrimonious conflict.

Knocking on Death's Door

By 2020, I was facing ruin and had to confront the prospect of firing over one hundred employees and advisors who had no involvement in the underlying events. That was the worst part: if this really meant the end of InSight, it wasn't just me who was going under. It was a lot of people who depended on me for their livelihood.

Maybe you've heard of the "Karpman drama triangle." First postulated by Dr. Stephen Karpman, it's a model of relationship transactions that posits there are three roles: the victim, the perpetrator, and the rescuer. These roles are not fixed; one can pivot between three points on a triangle. Edith and Fernando were perpetrators, who violated their clients' trust and caused them great financial loss, but instead of owning up to it, they chose to adapt the role of rescuer and collude to sue me instead. Those clients—the victims—thus became perpetrators by participating in an unfair and baseless claim against me and my business. As Karpman hypothesizes, the victim feels powerless and thus can experience a desire to regenerate a feeling of power or control by becoming a perpetrator; my victimhood, they reason, gives me the prerogative to perpetrate on another.

> If this really meant the end of InSight, it wasn't just me who was going under. It was a lot of people who depended on me for their livelihood.

The crisis revealed to me some of the darker aspects of human nature.

And no "rescuer" was coming to save me. I'd have to save myself—or die trying.

CHAPTER 8

DESPERATE TIMES

I had five claims pending, and if I lost a single one, my business would not survive. Each claim involved a dollar amount that was more than the firm could bear. In addition, in four of those five claims, I had been named personally, which would force not only the company but *me* into bankruptcy. Total financial ruin, on top of a probably permanent sullying of my name and reputation.

The severity of the situation was undeniable. If I had any hope of making a comeback in the industry in which I had become a pariah, I had to notch a win, or at least a "draw"—a favorable settlement—in all of these cases. If I lost even one, I would be penniless, given the magnitude of the claims and the refusal of my insurance company to pay out. How would I ever earn a livelihood again?

It was a Herculean task.

I desperately needed a pause button. Was there one more white rabbit hidden somewhere in my magician's hat? Even magic seemed inadequate. What I needed was a miracle. An act of God.

But none was coming.

Racking my brain for a solution, I considered the prospect of Chapter 11 bankruptcy. The airlines, for example, have done it at various times in the past: they use the bankruptcy to restructure rather than fold. If I could get a judge to grant us Chapter 11, it would freeze litigation *and* suspend the looming termination of our clearing contract. But that idea ran into the wall when I learned that the Securities Investor Protection Act explicitly bars broker-dealers from filing for Chapter 11.

Desperately searching for a way out, I came up with some alternative plans. I'm not an attorney, but I have a pretty sharp legal mind, and I did a little "creative lawyering" in the half light of the office late one night. What if we formally bankrupted the *holding company* but not the broker-dealer? It was the tiniest of possible loopholes, but if we could convince a bankruptcy judge, it might satisfy our creditors and allow us to survive, or at the very least buy us some time.

I approached several attorneys with this plan until I found one who, despite some misgivings, was on board.

"It's never been done before," he told me. "There's no precedent. It's a Hail Mary play."

"Let's do it anyway. Snap the ball. I'm ready."

Unfortunately, just before the filing, that attorney abruptly quit. At the last minute, I had to scramble to find someone else who would represent me. The next attorney was unambiguous in his opposition to the strategy. "That guy is smoking dope," he said of the first lawyer. "It'll never work."

I consulted with a third attorney, but he concurred with the second one. Chapter 11 simply wasn't an option, any way you cut it. My Hail Mary would have been picked off in the end zone and run back for a TD.

There was always the option of Chapter 7 bankruptcy, but that meant total liquidation rather than reorganization. What's left of your business is stripped and sold for parts to pay the creditors. Bye-bye, the party's over.

So I decided not to file for bankruptcy at all.

In January, Pershing set a March 1, 2020, date to start unwinding the operation, and moreover, they announced they would withhold $750,000 of the firm's capital to protect themselves. This was the *tiro de gracia*—the kill shot, the one that would finish me off. And it's a grim image, but holding back that $750,000 felt like Pershing's attempt to shield themselves from the splash of blood when they finally pulled the trigger.

Meanwhile, on the home front, things continued to deteriorate. Jerry Schwartz, who had been unfailingly loyal during the whole saga, quit because the stress was affecting his health. Then Paul, my operations manager, quit. Various managers and reps alike headed for the exits. Myrna was distraught, to a point of tears. The ship, I thought, was sinking irrevocably. Nothing was going to unpunch that gaping hole in the hull of the *Titanic*.

I couldn't in good faith let Myrna be the captain of the ship when it went under. If I was going to close things down, it had to be me at the helm, even if it was just a symbolic gesture. I told her, "It's time for me to be Big Brother again," so she resigned, and I took over again. On January 20, 2020, I announced to the staff that the end was nigh. We had about five weeks to wind down before Pershing's deadline. Pershing was going to start eliminating credit (margin) to the clients, with the goal of March 31 being the last trading day, and clients would only be able to liquidate assets but not transact business regularly.

A feeling of solitude surrounded me. It was just me and God pretty much. There was something surreal about it. I don't want to sound dramatic, but I can only imagine it's akin to what a patient with a terminal disease experiences when their doctor announces sullenly that all treatment options have been exhausted. That's where I was. Thirty years of building a dream, and everything was about to be extinguished.

Just like the time when I was lost in the desert, I surrendered to my fate. I prayed, "Spirit, if this is meant to be the end, I accept. If not, send me help. I cannot do it alone." It was incredibly painful, because I'm a fighter by nature; waving the white flag is anathema to me. In each prior crisis I had faced, I had survived, thanks to my own tenacity plus a lot of grace. This time, my luck had run out.

Sobering though it was, it was also strangely peaceful. You do get some solace from giving in. I felt like at last I could stop scheming, planning, problem-solving. I wasn't *okay* with it, but I accepted the reality. I had given it my all, tried all I could, and from a glass-is-half-full point of view, I had rather miraculously managed to keep fighting for longer than anyone expected, given that Pershing's original termination date was in April 2019.

I was basically powerless, but I still did have one power that was all mine: the ability to resign myself to my fate and accept whatever was coming next.

––––––––––

Another meeting followed in which I announced that the firm would formally shut down on March 31, giving the reps and advisors about eight weeks to find new employment. It was an unhappy meeting, needless to say. I couldn't help but think of the first time I gathered everyone into that same room a couple years earlier, shortly after I took over as head of the company. The spirit of newness, vigor, and optimism that prevailed then contrasted bitterly with the funereal atmosphere of this day.

I trudged back to my office and closed the door. At that moment, the phone rang. It was my assistant, who had a caller on the line. "I have a Judith from Interactive Brokers who wants to talk to you." I was in no place to talk to anyone, so I told him to take a message.

Minutes later my direct line rang. I picked up, and the gentleman on the other end identified himself as Nicholas, also of Interactive Brokers. I told him, "Your colleague also just called." Nicholas said he was in Connecticut and Judith was in Florida. And did I have a minute?

Not really! But something told me to listen to what this man had to say.

Nicholas was scouting for new business, and he knew (since it was public record) that Precise Investment Management—a new firm I had incorporated a couple months before, as a kind of life raft where I could take my own clients if InSight sunk into the sea—was recently founded. He asked if I wanted custody with their firm.

"The only thing I really need right now is a clearing firm," I said. "You guys wouldn't happen to have one?"

"As a matter of fact, we just started one."

I gave him an honest rundown of my situation: besieged by litigation across multiple court venues including FINRA, a terminated clearing contract, and a planned closure of the firm in just eight weeks. I didn't have much to offer, but I did have one or two chips to bargain with. "If you guys back me up with this, I'll give you a gateway to the Latin American market. Are you interested?" He said yes. He's a salesman—what else is he going to say?

I asked him to talk to his legal team and see if we could work it out.

To their credit, they came back and told me, "Carlos, we believe you that you're not a criminal and a fraudster. We're willing to give you a clearing contract." They put it in writing and sent it to Pershing (since Pershing had control of the accounts). Pershing was incredulous that someone had actually agreed to serve as my clearinghouse, but Interactive Brokers confirmed to Pershing that their offer was in fact legitimate.

In just a couple of days, I had managed to do what I hadn't been able to for the past year. Pershing agreed to give me an extension, with some limitations.

And just like that, I went from saying farewell to scrambling to restore some of my now-bare-bones staff. I called Paul and said, "I need an operations manager. Would you come back?" He agreed. That felt so sweet because he didn't even hesitate. I also had to convince the reps to accept the clearing agreement and to stay on. There was still $40 million in claims against me being fought bitterly in FINRA arbitration and in court. And I needed to deal with Pershing holding $750,000 of the firm's money.

But no matter what, this development offered a ray of hope in an otherwise dark period.

Another setback happened when Nick Iavarone's wife passed away and he had to temporarily withdraw from representing me. I had to quickly find a replacement attorney, a substitute counselor I didn't know well. The first hearing was scheduled for the last week of April 2020.

Obviously, the financial situation of the company was dire. We were burning through cash with basically no money coming in. But even more than capital, what I really needed was *time*. A moment of reprieve. If only God could reach down and make everything stand still.

Well, no one could have seen it coming, but that's exactly what happened next.

CHAPTER 9

BACK FROM THE BRINK

My friends and family all know I'm a huge fan of the *Star Trek* franchise, especially the movies. In a couple of the *Star Trek* films, the characters are put to the test in a "Kobayashi Maru," a no-win scenario. For example, in one, Kirk rigs the computer so that the simulated challenge Saavik has to undertake can't actually be beaten. The point of the exercise is not to find a solution but to see how the cadet handles failure. It's a test of character rather than problem-solving.

By February 2020, I felt like the Captain Kirk of the universe had put me in some kind of Kobayashi trial, where instead of looking for the exit, the only proper response was to stay cool under fire. I was all out of options. Catastrophic failure was looming. And the fact that other people (my reps, my employees, company leaders who I had worked with since the Horwitz days, my own sister even) were being impacted made it worse. People had stuck by me, trusted me, and now we were going belly up, despite recent positive developments.

Then March 2020 arrived. I don't need to remind you what happened then. It was a month that no one who lived through it will ever forget. As COVID-19 spread like wildfire, first throughout Asia, then Europe, and now North America, in the span of just a few weeks, the whole world ground to a halt by the first major pandemic since the Spanish flu of 1918. COVID shut down business, education, sports, entertainment—and, to my great fortune, the court system.

The coronavirus was the mother of all reprieves.

Now, I don't want to make light of the tragedy or talk about it in positive terms because the pandemic ravaged lives and livelihoods. It was (and remains, as I write this) a global tragedy. My family, too, has been affected by it. But at the time, I was in desperate need of any kind of lucky break. And when it became obvious that the COVID genie was not going to be stuffed back into the bottle, causing all human activity to pause, it jammed up the gears of the legal system.

I thought about the bleakest moment of my near-death crisis in the desert, the moment just before Mario and his dog appeared like a mirage in the darkness. COVID was a little like that. A "Marionavirus," if you will.

> It was like in the movies when the hero acquires a magical ability to stop time. The world froze, but I was still moving. The bullies were stuck in place, but I could punch back.

Before the lockdown, I was talking to my mom, who was in tears over what was happening to me and the firm. "It's a bunch of bullies kicking you while you're on the ground!" she said. And she was distraught that she could do nothing to protect me.

But suddenly, it was like in the movies when the hero acquires a magical ability to stop time. The world froze, but I was still moving. The bullies were stuck in place, but I could punch back.

FINRA, following suit with the rest of the world, announced that all proceedings would be suspended, and rescheduled on dates to be determined. No one knew the lockdown would drag on for so long or when business as usual would resume. I thought, "I don't know how long this reprieve will last. But I better make use of it."

Meanwhile, Pershing was stuck with us, which meant that their impending date on which they would sever ties would be pushed back a little, thus buying me more time to sell the new plan to the reps. I didn't know if Interactive would work out since they were new and unproven. But I had some breathing room.

Carlos's Counteroffensive

Until now, I had mostly been on the receiving end of the legal and financial punches flying at me from all directions. *El luchador* on the ropes. And as I mentioned earlier, I would only be able to pull through if I managed to score a win or a draw (i.e., a reasonable settlement) in each "match."

Now it was time to hit back.

One problem was that everyone was suing me in FINRA with no real cost to themselves, since of course the broker cannot make a counterclaim in that venue. I figured if I could raise the stakes for my adversaries, they would have something to lose by facing me. I had to hit 'em where it hurts, which meant, as is usually the case with such disputes, in the pocketbook.

For my first counterpunch, I sued Fernando, Rossi, and Epstein for fraud, on two grounds: (1) that hiding the sale of Biscayne to Epstein was a sham, and (2) for trying to make me cover the money that went to cover Rossi's overdraft at Deutsche Bank. This was the same suit I mentioned in chapter 7. This suit gave me some leverage:

it signaled that if you come after me, then I'm going to come after you twice as hard. The counterruck in rugby is a very effective move.

But nothing's ever easy when it comes to litigation. First, I'd have to serve each of them—and these three were a particularly slippery bunch.

Rossi, despite being a foreign national, was easy to serve as he had an attorney in the United States. But Fernando was in Argentina. In order to serve a party in a foreign jurisdiction, you normally have to go through a cumbersome process that involves the US Justice Department, which then reaches out to the Argentine authorities, and the whole thing can take up to a year. Which is ridiculous, if you think about it, in an era when a text message or email can speed five times around the world in the time it takes you to read this sentence.

That got me thinking: Why *can't* we serve someone digitally? I asked Nick, who by now had returned as my attorney following his period of bereavement, "What if we serve him via WhatsApp?" The app has a "read receipt" feature that shows you when the recipient opens a message (in the form of two blue tick marks next to the message).

There had been some precedent about serving through email, but it was still a gray area in case law. Well, what did we have to lose? Nick filed a motion that included an extensive explanation for the judge about what WhatsApp is and how it had been used in India and New Zealand to serve defendants. The judge granted the motion.

I sent a WhatsApp message to Fernando with the complaint, he opened it (the coveted blue check marks!), and I registered this in court. And to my knowledge, it was the first time a party in the United States had been served via WhatsApp. I took some pride in this fact. In the fight to clear my name, we were also creating legal precedent in some small way.

We eventually arrived at a settlement, in which Rossi would get a little money from my insurance carrier, I would drop the suit against them, and we would mutually do a walkaway of the "missing" funds that were transferred from InSight to Deutsche Bank via the fraudulent transfer instructions. However, that settlement, as I mentioned, fell through when the insurer refused to pay out. So it was still pending. But my counterattack strategy was at least providing some much-needed leverage.

Edith and Akerman

Edith, you recall, was the promoter of the lawsuit litigated by the firm Akerman. I took a two-pronged approach: I had to attack Edith directly as the instigator and conspirator. First, I filed a defamation suit against her in federal court, on the grounds that she had defamed me to her clients, with whom she was colluding to sue me for the fraud *she* had perpetrated.

Akerman was the firm that was also representing a total of 120 claimants (former clients of Biscayne) seeking $30 million in damages from both me and Raymond James. Of all the suits, that was the most menacing, just because of the staggering dollar amount. And mind you, this was not a class action; I would have to face each claimant individually, which meant hefty legal expenses. Nick estimated I'd be ponying up around $800,000 to fight these cases, not to mention endless hours of paperwork and prep. So the best-case scenario was that, even if I won, I would have been almost a million in the hole just in legal fees. And imagine if the FINRA arbitrators ended up ruling against me, even for just a fraction of the $30 million. Even ten cents on the dollar would have cost me $3 million, which was money I didn't have, since insurance wasn't going to cover it.

In a different lawsuit, Rossi was suing Amicorp, which was the legal owner of the issuers of the fraudulent notes. And Akerman, remember, was *also* Amicorp's legal counsel—playing both ends, representing the clients who had been screwed over by being sold those notes but also defending the owners of those notes. One of these legal actions was playing out in court and the other in arbitration, but it really looked like Akerman was buttering both sides of the bread.

Normally, that would be problematic. In court there are "sanctions," or you can file a motion to disqualify counsel, but you can't do that in FINRA. The arbitration panel has no jurisdiction over the attorneys because they aren't members of FINRA, which gives attorneys quite a lot of leeway to do whatever they want.

Seeking a way around this, I laid a trap for Akerman. I sued Amicorp in Illinois district court seeking indemnity for the FINRA complaint that Akerman had filed against me. I was claiming, "I'm not responsible. The owner of the fraudulent notes, Amicorp, is responsible." Akerman, naturally, emerged to defend Amicorp, their client.

Once Akerman did that, it gave me grounds to then sue *Akerman* to disqualify them (on the basis of conflict of interest) from representing Edith and Biscayne's defrauded clients in their suit against me.

That was the trap, and they fell into it, like a predator outsmarted by his prey.

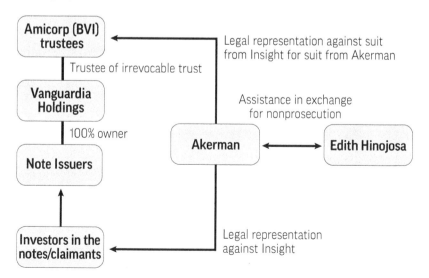

By maneuvering in this fashion, I left Akerman in a difficult position. Were I to prevail in my lawsuit, Akerman would be disqualified. Even if I failed, and Akerman proceeded with the suit against me, it would probably be for naught because I was teetering on bankruptcy, and I knew they were aware of this. In other words: you screw me, and I'll screw you.

That was my attempt to gain leverage to finagle a settlement. Time would tell if it worked.

The Gift That Keeps on Giving

In a saga full of labyrinthine twists and turns, there was one surprise that proved to be the best of all.

Francisco Rodriguez, the Akerman attorney working on the case, is good at bringing the business to the firm, but that's it. He was either bamboozled by Edith or in cahoots with her with full eyes open. I don't know, and at the end I don't really care.

In the process of discovery, we demanded all communications between the claimants and Edith. They hemmed and hawed, claiming that communications between Biscayne and clients were privileged and thus not subject to discovery, but in the end they were required to cough them up. Instead of giving us only those communications, Edith had given them her server, and they just gave us the whole thing.

Thus, Akerman provided 350,000 documents, including information that did not involve Akerman's clients.

My legal team and I had been sifting through this trove for months now. But then we found something that turned the case on its head: an audio recording of a phone call between Edith and some of her clients that we hadn't seen before. In that call, Edith is explaining that they needed to come up with evidence of malfeasance in order to sue me and my firm, and that such evidence was lacking: "What do we need to frame them? ... We need them to pay—that's it—and if one cannot afford it, someone else has to pay," she said, according to the translation. (In Spanish, "*Que es lo que necesitamos para inculpar? Necesitamos que paguen.... Y no puede pagar uno, tiene que pagar el otro.*")

I practically jumped for joy when this came to light, because it was as close as we would get to a smoking gun exposing the malicious intent of our adversaries—namely, that InSight was being set up as the fall guy, the scapegoat, for the misdeeds of bigger players.

> *We need them to pay us and I include myself because you know my position. We need them to pay, that's it, and if one cannot afford it, somebody else has to pay.* <u>*What do we need to make the ones that can afford, like Raymond James, InSight, not recognize these numbers?*</u> *As the lawyer said, there is not enough evidence... So, I told them, but they continued selling, this is an important proof of evidence. We need to hold on that to make things work.*

A Strange Day in Bankruptcy Court

Edith is the classic Icarus figure: someone with grand ambitions who flies too close to the sun and is knocked back to earth by her own hubris. Hubris is a little too charitable—"greed" might be a more accurate term. In any event, she is an interesting figure.

Born and raised in Ecuador, she started her career at Citibank, without a college degree. I guess the company saw her as a worthwhile asset because they paid for her college education, and she graduated with a business degree. Later she jumped from Citi to Bear Stearns, and meanwhile established a small company in Quito with her daughter and several other associates. When Bear Stearns imploded in the 2008 financial crisis, she went to work for Allen Stanford's company (which also operated a Ponzi). That's when she was recruited by Biscayne.

I have no way of knowing whether Edith knew the worthless notes were fraudulent at the time she sold them, but I do know this: she is, for better or worse, a gifted saleswoman. And wittingly or not, her aggressive selling of those notes was integral in sustaining Biscayne's Ponzi scheme.

She has also been, to my knowledge, dogged by all kinds of legal problems in Ecuador too, which is not the subject of this book, but it certainly adds a dramatic wrinkle to her colorful life. She owned (or owns) a nice hotel with her husband in the mountains in Ecuador. And she got sued locally by one of her clients and somehow got arrested and was released with an ankle bracelet and instructions not to leave the country. I had to go through the complicated process of serving her there, but by that time, she had fled Ecuador.

How was she able to do so? I don't know that either. The borders in Latin America are a little more porous than other places. Perhaps she bribed someone to remove the ankle bracelet and transited over a land border, to Peru or Colombia, and then onward from there.

Anyway, I was trying to track her down in order to serve her. I knew she was a permanent resident of the United States, and I suspected she may have fled to Florida, where she had ties (for example, an Orlando phone number was linked to her).

I hired a PI to track her down. After eight months of searching, I finally found her in Orlando, and she was served with the lawsuit there. The day she was obligated to respond in court, she filed for bankruptcy in Florida Central District, claiming she was destitute, having overspent all her credit cards, and was unable even to make the next car payment. I knew this was untrue. It seemed like her bankruptcy filing was a naked ploy to dodge my suit.

I had to find a bankruptcy lawyer, who told me there would be a 341 hearing, which I should attend because that's when the petitioners (Edith among them) plead their case to the bankruptcy trustee. If the trustee grants the petitioner's request to discharge the debt, then creditors can't touch the bankrupt person's remaining assets, which would mean my lawsuit against her would be toast.

I hired an Ecuadorian investigative agency called Fextor to do some digging, and they hit pay dirt. They learned that she had been investigated by the financial authorities in Ecuador, and we managed to obtain reports showing that she had substantial assets in Ecuador, documents that I brought to the courthouse.

A surreal scene ensued. In bankruptcy court, the claimants are called by the trustee and asked to state how much they owe. The judge says, "Is there any creditor here who objects to the discharge?" Usually no one objects because most of the people there are just trying to discharge small amounts (relatively speaking) of debt in the four or five figures, often consumer credit card debt. Small potatoes type of cases. The "discharge" is usually granted, and the petitioner gets sent to debt counseling.

Then the judge called Edith's name. She was there with her husband and her attorney. She was dressed in jeans and a polo and Skechers tennis shoes, the ones that look like platform shoes to make you look taller. She had the air of a shoplifter who thinks she's getting away with it as she walks out the door with an armful of stolen merchandise.

"How much do you owe?" the judge asked.

"Around $5,000," she said.

"Why are you filing for bankruptcy?"

"I make too little money, and I overspend."

"Is there any creditor who objects to this discharge?"

"Me!" I said.

The face she made when she saw me object was priceless, like the face the shoplifter makes when they get busted by the security guard with one foot out the door. She and I had never met.

The trustee asked me to come forward and sit next to her.

"How much does she owe you?"

"Four million dollars."

The trustee almost fell out of her chair.

Edith claimed she was working for minimum wage in a day care center. This from the woman who once earned millions in commissions for an investment firm. Was it possible she really was broke? Perhaps. Probable? No. I suspected she was pretending to lead a destitute life. It wouldn't be too hard to maintain the facade in America seeing as how she still had significant assets in her home country.

"It's a ruse," I argued. "She fled Ecuador. Here's a report from the financial intel agency detailing her assets in Ecuador. She colluded with her clients to frame me."

Edith denied it, naturally. But her bankruptcy petition was rejected.

I won the battle that day, short-circuiting her ploy.

Moreover, this case proved useful in other ways.

In FINRA arbitration, the panel only has jurisdiction over FINRA members. Edith and Fernando are not subject to FINRA jurisdiction, which made it convenient for their clients to file arbitrations against me because Edith and Fernando were out of reach of FINRA's claws. Which also meant that I could not subpoena them in the FINRA case to produce documents. Documents that are produced in a FINRA arbitration are subject to a confidentiality agreement.

However, in the bankruptcy case, I *could* subpoena third parties to disclose relevant information. And the bankruptcy court's subpoena superseded FINRA's confidentiality agreement. This way, the 350,000 documents related to Edith that Akerman coughed up also became available to me in my cases in other venues outside FINRA.

In other words, the documents I introduced into the bankruptcy proceedings became a matter of public record, so now I could use those in my defense in other cases.

So ironically, her bankruptcy filing was a big break for me: what she had intended as a measure to hide behind bankruptcy law became an opening in which I could charge through and counterattack using fresh ammo.

Suing FINRA

That development was great news. When you're buried in an avalanche of litigation, the slightest reprieve can feel like a major win. But just as quickly, the next assault is coming for you.

It's like swimming in rough waters: you dive through one big wave as it breaks over your head, but that gives you only enough time to come to the surface, take a gulp of air, and prepare for the next wave as it starts to crest.

Suddenly, in the summer of 2020, FINRA announced that arbitrations, which had been suspended when the nation went into lockdown, would be started up again via Zoom.

I immediately balked at the idea of litigating over Zoom since it would be detrimental to my defense. For one thing, one of the key issues involved ascertaining the authenticity of signatures, something that is much better to do in person, when you can look at physical copies of signatures with your own eyeballs. In addition, it was a complex case involving multiple individuals, foreign language translators, and likely weeks of hearings. It just wasn't feasible to do it on Zoom.

Jenice Malecki (the attorney for the plaintiffs) filed a motion that she wanted to proceed on Zoom. We objected but the panel agreed with her and scheduled a mid-August hearing date. Nick concurred with me it was outrageous to do this over Zoom. And I was adamant. Moreover, I had FINRA's own rules and regulations on my side. The arbitration protocol to which FINRA was beholden dictated in writing that any arbitration hearing must be held at the place and time designated by FINRA's director of arbitration. That was the rule in black and white. Where does it say he or she has the power to hold *virtual* hearings?

So we decided to sue FINRA to stay the Zoom hearing, arguing that this was a violation of FINRA's contract between its members, and not merely a technical one either. Conducting hearings in person is substantially different than conducting them via video conference.

Granted, it was a risky move to sue your own regulator. But what did I have to lose?

We filed in Illinois district court. I can only imagine the pearl clutching that took place when FINRA was served. *A lowly member, sue us? The horror!* Talk about chickens coming home to roost. Justice is a two-way street.

Anyway, district court set a date, both sides appeared and argued our respective position, and since the parties could not agree, the court ordered mediation. They designated a court-appointed mediator. It felt good to see FINRA attorneys forced to come to the table (figuratively speaking; we did it on the phone) and negotiate with me, on equal terms.

I maintained that if FINRA wanted to change their rules governing the time and place of hearings, they would have to file with the SEC first. (FINRA is a quasi-independent entity but is subject to the jurisdiction of the SEC.) If they formally got permission by the

SEC, then sure, they could conduct Zoom meetings. Otherwise, it was a breach of the contract.

We went back and forth with the mediator. No agreement was reached. It went back to the judge, who handed down his ruling, which was that FINRA was not a party to an arbitration agreement (neither claimant or respondent), they were just the referee, and hence there was no breach of contract. So I lost this round.

I considered appealing, but by the time the appeal would have been heard, the FINRA Zoom hearing would have already transpired. So I had to concede.

In rugby sometimes you "concede the ruck"—the opposing team turns over the ball, and you look to the next play to get back at them.

But our efforts attracted some attention in the legal and financial press because the question of whether and how to conduct legal proceedings over Zoom was suddenly a big issue now that the pandemic was forcing courthouses to shut down. I know I wasn't the only one to object to conducting important legal business via an app and a tiny screen. We lost in our motion, but I take solace in the fact that no one else had the cojones to take on FINRA in this way. And later, quietly, in the middle of the night, FINRA changed the rule giving discretion to the panel to hold virtual hearings. I took this as FINRA agreeing with me that they had violated their own rule but were too proud to admit it.

The Next Showdown

Jenice Malecki was the attorney on three arbitrations against me: two from the Rossi family and one from an unrelated client of Fernando who we can call "J."

"J's" arbitration was the one I sued FINRA over. The arbitration was going to go forward by Zoom starting in mid-August 2020. I decided that I was going to participate from my attorney's office. Even if it was done on Zoom, at least I would be in the same room as counsel to talk when we would go on break.

Day one, I get on Zoom, and there they were: multiple squares on my screen, and three of them (the arbitrators) held my firm's existence in their hands. I saw Malecki, who I had met once before, sitting in her office in New York.

Successful Roman generals always preferred to pick the time and the place of the battle. It had been two years since she filed the first arbitration, I had been trying to postpone the confrontation until I was on more solid footing, but those same generals also knew that picking the time and place of a battle is a luxury most of us don't have. I was finally going to go head-to-head with the woman who, without meeting me once, decided to tar and feather my name in order to get into Pershing's pocket.

I had to stay cool, which was hard after what she had put me through. I was playing the long game though, and if it meant being on my best behavior so be it.

Jerry Schwartz told me once, "These claimants' attorneys are nothing more that glorified actors," and I confirmed it during a previous arbitration, when opposing counsel burst into tears in the middle of closing arguments. They come at you guns blazing when they file the arbitration, hoping the broker-dealer will settle before hearing. They rarely have experience actually litigating.

Malecki portrayed herself as the champion for the little guy, but she had to contend with the original sin of her engagement, that Fernando voluntarily gave her those communications and that she was counsel for Rossi's company that received the unauthorized transfers. She was playing both ends against the middle, and in the hearing she would have to explain what Fernando would get in exchange for those communications, and also why Rossi's company was entitled to keep the benefit of the stolen assets.

We requested all communications between that claimant ("J") and Fernando, and when I got the records, something about it seemed fishy. In particular, the last communication between Fernando and J (who alleged that Fernando screwed him out of $2 million) was just an email that said, "Fernando, give me a call." The absence of other communications suggested to me that some documents were being withheld. If someone cheats you out of a couple million, there's going to be a few irate exchanges about that fact, right? The last message you send to the swindler is unlikely to be an offhand "Give me a call."

In FINRA arbitration, we asked for a forensic analysis of communications since I thought they were leaving stuff out. The panel denied my motion. But later, more communications came out during discovery. And the substance of those communications was akin to Edith's exchanges with her clients. Fernando never said, "Let's frame InSight," but there was a lot of behind-the-scenes "buck passing" and scapegoating to make me the fall guy, once again—don't come after me, let's go after Carlos together, blah blah blah. Different lyrics, same tune.

Now Malecki had some 'splainin' to do. I saw my opening and using the balance of the insurance policy we were able to negotiate a settlement and make client "J" go away.

Another one gone, three to go.

Shadows

By the end of 2020, including the suits *I* had filed in my counterattack strategy, I was dealing with nineteen different legal actions, enough to make your head spin. I couldn't keep up, both in time and money (legal fees).

In Jungian psychoanalysis, there is a concept of "the shadow," which Jung described as that part of ourselves we reject, repress, deny, or hide. We all have it. Often the shadow is tied to childhood— what the child's mind does to cope with reality or trauma. The shadow is real, and it can't just be ignored. It creates suffering, if not examined.

In my case, somewhere in childhood I think I somehow internalized the notion, maybe from the unusual relationship between my mom and dad, that I was a mistake, a failure. And many of my life struggles have been tied to this. I think it also accounts for my lifelong impulse (for better or worse) to tilt at windmills. That's why I've always been so driven; I'm trying to prove to myself by being successful that I am not a mistake. I was so afraid of failing because it would prove my shadow right: "See, you were a mistake, and that's why you failed." And that's the trap: shadow is a void that cannot be filled with material rewards or professional success or anything like that.

Another aspect of my shadow is the way I deal with pain: I bury it where it's hard to "access." If you punch me in the face, I wanna punch back, but then I start walking away and say, "What happened? Nothing. It's just a scratch. I don't remember."

The experience from February 2020, when I was facing the no-win scenario, looking into the abyss, was so painful. I didn't know how to process it or access it. I just wanted to pass through the pain. Once I sat with it and allowed myself to feel, well, it was really hard.

Freedom comes only from detachment to outcome, from the knowledge that I was not a mistake, successful or not. When I had no way out, no more rabbits in the hat, I had to surrender to the possibility of failing. But failure in my business did not mean that I was a failure on a deeper level, and the acceptance of this truth was the catharsis I needed. They say, "Jump into the void, and the net will appear," and that is what I did. I accepted my fate, and in that moment is when the net "magically appeared."

CHAPTER 10

OUT OF THE DESERT

The legal slugfest continued as I slogged through the latter half of 2020.

I still had a pile of arbitrations to deal with. But at last, the tactical moves I made were bearing fruit, and things were starting to break my way.

The biggest source of anxiety was still the 120 claimants (defrauded Biscayne account holders) whose complaints were being litigated by Akerman. In those cases, Raymond James and InSight were defendants. But tucked away in the trove of 350,000 documents was that damning recording by Edith colluding with her bamboozled clients to turn their ire—and their legal firepower—onto me.

Edith's blunder had given me an ace up my sleeve. It wasn't much, but it was enough leverage to bring Akerman to the negotiating table. I told them, "When we go into arbitration, I'm going to play this recording before the panel, and FINRA is going to see that this whole case is a frame-up job. And if you lose in arbitration, I still intend to proceed with my suit against your client in court!"

Remember that while Akerman was litigating claims against me in FINRA, I was suing both Akerman (based on conflict of interest / breach of fiduciary duty) *and* Akerman's client Amicorp (seeking damages equal to the amount Amicorp was seeking from me). Meanwhile, Raymond James was named alongside my company as a codefendant in the case pursued by Akerman. Technically speaking, these were two different matters—FINRA complaints against me, and my suit against Amicorp. Akerman was involved in both, so pursuing both would (if I were to prevail) put them in a bind.

So the people at Akerman, shrewd attorneys and businesspeople (a law firm is after all a business) that they are, had to weigh the impact of one or the other.

What Akerman sought for its clients was, of course, a big payout to compensate them for their financial loss. But I was basically tapped out—even my insurance was running on empty. However, Raymond James, one of the biggest financial services companies in the world, has deep pockets. So if FINRA tossed that case because of Edith's inculpatory phone recording, *or* if I prevailed in my district court suit to disqualify Akerman as counsel, it would have meant a blown opportunity for Akerman to keep litigating the FINRA complaint and collect a hefty settlement on behalf of its clients, if not from me then from Raymond James.

Basically, Akerman was in a jam because they were pursuing two mutually exclusive goals (such is the nature of a conflict of interest). I can only presume that it created discord among Akerman's partners, as some were advocating for the Biscayne clients while others were fighting for Amicorp. My countersuits against the parties had muddled what was an already complicated situation for them.

My offer, therefore, was simple: settle the FINRA complaint

CHAPTER 10: OUT OF THE DESERT

against me for whatever amount of money I have left in my insurance policy, and I'll withdraw my lawsuit against your clients. The Akerman lawyers said, "We have to speak to our clients and see if they'll accept." But I knew the clients would go along with whatever their attorneys encouraged.

And sure enough, we agreed on a settlement, which drained the rest of my insurance but spared me from paying a lot of money out of pocket. I considered it a victory, especially considering that before I had been looking at $30 million in damages. Not only was that a staggering amount of money, but it had been the biggest black mark on my name. And now it was, for all intents and purposes, gone.

It seemed that my strategy of being the obnoxious mosquito buzzing around the elephant's ass was working. Or to use a different analogy, it's like guerilla warfare: when you're a ragtag band of rebels facing a much larger adversary, you won't win in a conventional confrontation. You won't overpower them, so you must identify their few weak points and concentrate all your strength there. In essence, you have to use your small size as an asset—your rival has more to lose, and you can bend them to your will just by being an annoyance. Create enough chaos and confusion to drive them to the negotiating table, just to get rid of you since they have bigger targets anyway.

Inching Forward with Interactive

That settlement also had one important side benefit: it paved the way to secure the clearing contract with Interactive Brokers. Immediately, we got to work converting the accounts from Pershing to Interactive. However, we soon realized that while Interactive was a fantastic platform for some things, it wasn't ideal for providing the full range of services our clients were used to receiving.

In life, it often happens that when things go wrong, they go *really* wrong —the whole "when it rains, it pours" thing. And that was how

> In life, it often happens that when things go wrong, they go *really* wrong

things had gone for me throughout most of 2019 and 2020. But the universe, I believe, is fair: this dynamic works the other way too, and sometimes, one lucky break follows another even when you think you've burned off your reserve of good fortune. Divine intervention swoops in to push you out of the way of the moving train.

As we were struggling to figure out how to do business using Interactive's system, out of the blue I got a call from a gentleman from Axos Clearing, Roy DiMaria. I had actually made contact with the company a long time ago, when I was scrambling for a replacement for Pershing. Those were the dark days when I was untouchable in the industry, and *no one* wanted to work with me.

So in the intervening years, I forgot about Axos Clearing. But now they were calling again. "Hey Carlos, I'm just checking up on you," said Roy. "How is it going with the litigation?"

I told him how I had just settled the biggest case, which constituted three-quarters of the claims against me. I was no longer persona non grata; the dark cloud was lifting. And fortunately, while some clearinghouses require exclusivity, Interactive did not. So I was able to negotiate a second clearing contract with Axos that, in combination with Interactive Brokers, allowed me to plug the gaps and basically provide everything that Pershing had provided us.

I had to laugh at this turn of events: one moment I had zero clearing contracts, the next moment I had two! And this all happened within a span of eight weeks, after two years of wandering in the wilderness, desperate for help.

The dual arrangement became a juggling act, and the conversion required some intricate planning. But I could finally free myself of dependency on Pershing.

The Battle Rages On

Meanwhile, I was still dealing with arbitrations involving Edith and Fernando's clients.

By now it was autumn 2020, a tumultuous season for the entire nation. The contentious presidential campaign was drawing to a close. Multiple cities and regions were struggling with their second wave of COVID. Wildfires were torching swaths of California. The Black Lives Matter demonstrations for racial justice that started in May 2020, while more subdued, persisted.

As for me, I had depleted my insurance money by settling the arbitrations, and I had three to go.

"Well, God will provide," I thought. I just had to maintain faith and keep fighting.

We moved most of the accounts out of Pershing by the end of September. FINRA forced me to start the second of the Malecki arbitrations in December 2020. It was déjà vu all over again because I had spent three weeks in front of her already, and now we were back, litigating the same issues once again.

This time it was the complaint involving "Raul" Rossi (Diego Rossi's father-in-law) and Fernando, wherein Raul's money had been transferred to Deutsche Bank to the benefit of Diego after Fernando overdrafted the account. Fernando was the culprit here—so why wasn't Rossi suing *him* rather than us? Or the father-in-law should have gone after his son-in-law to get the father-in-law's money back. But I guess they didn't want to do that because then the son-in-law would still owe

Deutsche Bank. Everyone was just constantly trying to pass the buck and leave some other party (InSight, in particular) on the hook for the fraudulent transfer that never should have taken place.

It was a total racket.

I suspected that they were protecting Fernando after cutting some sort of deal with him to go after me instead. Maybe they saw me as an easier target.

I wanted Diego Rossi to testify and explain why he was entitled to keep money that had been fraudulently transferred from another account (his relative's account), thus forcing us to reimburse his relative. We got no answers from the other side, just a lot of "I don't knows" and "I don't recalls." We also managed to obtain testimony of two Deutsche Bank executives stating that they received clear instructions that these securities were for someone else, so how did they end up in Rossi's account?

One problem with FINRA arbitration is people can lie without being charged with perjury.

Claimants' attorneys work on what is called a contingency basis, meaning that they work for a percentage of whatever their client gets from an award or settlement, and if there isn't one, the attorney has worked for free. This is why they prefer the extortion approach: maximum return for minimum effort.

Given that my insurance money was gone, I decided to make Malecki work for her money. She had told one of my attorneys, "That Carlos is a hothead. I will make him explode in front of the panel," so my plan was to turn myself into the most boring professor you have had in school. Slow the process; put everyone to sleep. She kept me on the stand for ten consecutive days, and she was obviously frustrated, to the point one day that she started yelling at me. Talk about a hothead! I decided to pull the transcript and print her irate quotes on T-shirts that I then circulated to my legal team. Heck, you gotta have fun somehow. It then became a game of "see who can get the next T-shirt quote."

Divine intervention struck again. Recall that I had sued Rossi and Fernando in district court for colluding to induce me to reimburse them for money lost to Deutsche Bank. Unsurprisingly, they had filed a motion to dismiss the case, based on various grounds. But during the FINRA hearing that was taking place now, the district court judge denied their motion to dismiss and ordered the case to proceed.

It was good timing because now Rossi had something to lose,

since I was suing him for the amount of money that the panel would have awarded him if I ended up losing the FINRA case. Different cases, different venues, but ones that nonetheless had indirect bearing on each other. My "parallel suit" gave me some ammo.

So once again, we entered into settlement negotiations. Unfortunately, the fact that I had no more insurance money gave me very little wiggle room in terms of arriving at a settlement figure I could actually pay. But wouldn't you know it? The universe smiled on me again in the form of another out-of-the-blue phone call. For a long time, the sound of the phone would often give me a jolt of anxiety, so frequently did it herald bad news on the other end. But now, with all these fortuitous calls coming in, I was starting to welcome its ring!

This time, it was the owner of Banco San Juan Internacional. We had first spoken when I was trying to sell InSight when the walls were caving in. He didn't bid, but we established a good rapport. Since that time, he had also been through a trial by fire during which the bank was shut down for a while by federal regulators. But he had resolved those issues and was in good standing again, ready to do business. We were both in rebuilding mode.

In fact, he was calling to offer me a position on the board of his bank. He was surprised to learn that I was still in business, figuring that all the litigation would have forced me into bankruptcy by now.

I said, "Thank you for the offer. I would be happy to serve on the board, but I'm not dead yet!"

What I needed more than anything was capital, and I asked him if he'd be willing to loan me $800,000. He agreed.

With that offer in hand, I went back to Malecki and made her an offer: if she withdrew the arbitration, I'd withdraw my case in federal court. In the end, we resolved the remaining Fernando litigation in a way that was favorable to all parties.

Ultimately, Malecki did a great disservice to her client Rossi. By playing both sides against the middle (representing the entity that received the benefit of the transfers and the clients that lost the assets) and not suing Fernando, she allowed Deutsche Bank to run off with the stolen money. Instead of suing Pershing and me, her clients would have been better off if she had represented them in a claim against Deutsche Bank. This would not have recovered all the money, but it would've been a much better outcome than what Rossi and his family ended with.

In any event, with the resolution of that case, I reached an important symbolic milestone: for the first time, the number of cases in which I was the plaintiff outweighed the number of cases in which I was the defendant.

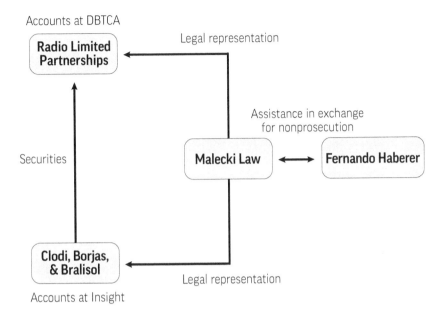

Accounts at DBTCA

Radio Limited Partnerships

Legal representation

Assistance in exchange
for nonprosecution

Securities

Malecki Law

Fernando Haberer

Clodi, Borjas,
& Bralisol

Legal representation

Accounts at Insight

Russian Roulette

I've insisted upon my innocence since the first page of this book. So it's only reasonable for you to wonder, "If Carlos did nothing wrong, why did he settle so many cases instead of fighting them out?"

It's like this: Let's say someone offered you a million dollars to play a game of Russian roulette. They put a single bullet in a six-shooter and spin the cylinder. That means you have a five-in-six chance of becoming an instant millionaire—and a one-in-six chance of death.

When you face arbitration, civil action, or even a criminal trial, and your adversaries want to settle, you encounter a similar dilemma, regardless of your guilt or innocence. You can take the offer, knowing it's going to cost you, or you can try to go all-or-nothing by duking it out in court (or in FINRA arbitration, in my case).

So it's a huge gamble. And I had lost enough already. I didn't want to play Russian roulette with what was left of my career, my savings, and my name.

Factoring into this decision was the fact that, in FINRA, anything goes. Arbitration, in my opinion, is unfavorable to the defendant even though it is ostensibly neutral. And FINRA rules dictated that even if I appealed, I would need to close the firm due to lack of capital. If FINRA ruled against me and awarded money to the claimants for bogus reasons, there would have been nothing I could do.

FINRA arbitrators, it's worth mentioning, are not exactly Supreme Court justice–caliber legal experts. In fact they're unlikely to be legal professionals at all. According to FINRA's own website, they need not have any experience in either arbitration or the securities industry. "Applicants [to FINRA's arbitration program] should have at least five years of paid business and/or professional experience—inside or outside of the securities industry—and at least two years of college-level credits."[3] After just seven hours of training, they're eligible to hear cases![4] That doesn't sound like a high bar given the magnitude and complexity of some of the complaints. Now, to be fair, a FINRA panel adjudicating claims of more than $100,000 consists of three arbitrators. In the past, one of those was a "nonpublic" arbitrator with securities experience, but years ago FINRA got rid of the industry arbitrator. Moreover, arbitrators are notorious for granting "pity money" for claimants. Given all this, you can understand my skepticism about getting a fair hearing in kangaroo court, especially after everything I had been through.

So for the Rossi case, for example, I estimated I had only a one-in-ten chance of losing, so the odds were actually in my favor. I had the evidence I didn't do anything wrong. But if my number comes

---

3   "Basic Arbitrator Training (Modules 1-15)," FINRA, accessed January 4, 2022, https://www.finra.org/arbitration-mediation/basic-arbitrator-training-modules-1-15.

4   "Required Basic Arbitrator Training Program," FINRA, accessed January 4, 2022, https://www.finra.org/arbitration-mediation/required-basic-arbitrator-training.

up, the one out of ten, I'm dead! And if I lose—say, FINRA awards $6 million—I have to pay out some of that even if I appeal.

Plus there was the issue of time and legal expenses. Even if I won in the arbitrations, I would have had to exhaust more hours, plus I'd have to pay my attorneys to defend me. I was bleeding money and time, and fighting these multifront legal battles was preventing me from managing the company, recruiting advisors, winning new business—everything involved in my actual career. The litigations were a constant millstone around my neck.

So I made a pragmatic decision to save time and money and enjoy the peace of mind that came from putting these disputes to bed.

That's how I emerged, bruised and battered but alive, as 2020 passed into 2021. Inches from an untimely demise, I fought back against the darkness and held on long enough, until I found my way out of the desert and back on the road. And it was very good to be on the road again. Because it was a long, glorious road stretching into the future, and while I still had myriad problems to resolve, I'd get a chance to keep traveling, to see what lay beyond that magical, unknown place just beyond the horizon.

CHAPTER 11

DARKNESS AND LIGHT

The yin-yang is an ancient Chinese symbol consisting of a circle divided into halves (one white with a black dot in the middle, the other black with a white dot in the middle) by an S-curve in the middle. It represents many things, but in the simplest terms, it's a symbol  of duality. The juxtaposition of the black and white halves, with their respective white and black dots, means there is light in darkness and darkness in light. The totality of the universe consists of both. Nothing is absolute; everything also coexists alongside its antithesis.

It's a good way of summing up the whole three-year saga for me that began in October 2018 when I first received Pershing's termination letter. That period, which tested me in every way (intellectually, physically, emotionally, and of course spiritually), showed me both the ruthless Machiavellian side of human nature as well as the good and selfless kind. I faced off against people who were willing to destroy my life and career just to save themselves, but I was also carried through it thanks to the loyalty of my employees, advisors, and managers, many of whom stayed with me on blind faith. I don't know how they did it since they also have families to feed, and they stuck by me. That I'll never forget.

———

Yesterday I got a surprising email from a colleague. "Carlos, did you see this?" she wrote. It was a press release from the Department of Justice: "Three Operators of Financial Services Firm Charged and Arrested in Alleged $155 Million Investment Fraud Scheme."[5] Fernando, along with two of Biscayne's founders, was nabbed by federal agents for "conspiring to defraud investors and financial institutions as part of an international fraud scheme stretching through the United States, South America, and Europe ... [and] charged with conspiracy to commit wire fraud, conspiracy to commit bank fraud, and conspiracy to commit money laundering." (Gustavo Trujillo, meanwhile, is awaiting sentencing after pleading guilty to federal charges in a separate but related case.)

The gravity of those charges reminds me of what I went up against, and the outrageousness of Fernando, Edith, and others trying to pin their own, likely criminal, malfeasance on me still stings. Nevertheless, I'm trying my best to do what I call a "cut and bless": not celebrate that my adversaries are suffering, just relish the peace and the closure that has finally come while cutting these people out of my life, moving on, and hopefully forgetting about them.

———

5   "Three Operators of Financial Services Firm Charged and Arrested in Alleged $115 Million Investment Fraud Scheme," The United States Department of Justice, September 9, 2021, https://www.justice.gov/opa/pr/three-operators-financial-services-firm-charged-and-arrested-alleged-155-million-investment.

It feels good to be vindicated and to see the cloud around me starting to lift. To be purified of the stink that has clung to me. To be redeemed from the inflammatory language and the unfair characterizations and the accusations of being a grifter that dogged me for years. I am grateful that the world is seeing that I had nothing to do with this fraud, and in fact I was the one who helped bring it down! I just didn't mean for that house of cards to fall on top of *me*!

> It feels good to be vindicated and to see the cloud around me starting to lift.

Who knows how many more people would have been victimized if I hadn't blown the whistle then? For that I am proud. That's another silver lining.

Now, ironically, Edith (the number one seller of the bogus securities) is the only one who remains free. Maybe the prosecutors don't have enough evidence to bring charges; maybe they're slowly building a case and will come after her eventually. Only time will tell.

But she hasn't disappeared, at least. In fact, I actually deposed her (via Zoom) recently in connection with the ongoing bankruptcy case. She appeared with no attorney (he allegedly quit), and she is still maintaining the charade that she's penniless. During the hearing she put on an Oscar-caliber performance, crying and playing the victim. She still refuses to admit responsibility for any of this. She insists Biscayne individuals fooled her into selling the securities. I can't say for sure if she *knew* it was a Ponzi scheme from the beginning, though she certainly knew that the notes were not guaranteed by the Federal Reserve, despite telling her clients otherwise (based on what her clients have told me and also documented in emails obtained during the proceedings).

The truth is that while I intend to follow through on the bankruptcy case, I won't waste any more resources on pursuing her, like

Captain Ahab obsessively chasing the white whale. Eventually, Edith, too, will fade into the ether, and I can "cut and bless" her as well and focus on what really matters, what I wanted to do all along: run my business.

InSight Lives On

In November of 2020, the firm celebrated its fifty-year anniversary, going back to the Horwitz days. We survived by the skin of our teeth and are now working hard to rebuild and carve out a niche in the industry. I have grand ambitions, and I don't intend to let the setbacks of the past few years impede me.

My near-term goal is to rebuild our assets to the level they were at before the Biscayne fiasco, which reduced our size by a third. I've been in promising talks with a number of investors, and I've entered into a partnership with the owner of the Puerto Rican bank I mentioned before. Along with him and other investors, we're creating an exciting future together. Meanwhile, I'm bringing in new people, recruiting some advisors who left and hiring new ones.

InSight had been reduced to a beat-up car with missing parts but somehow, miraculously, was still running. So we've been installing new equipment, making upgrades, swapping out the old for the new, and restoring the vehicle to glory. What else would you expect from the proud grandson of a car junkyard owner?

Even ending the relationship with Pershing has proven to be a blessing in disguise. It was a setback at first, but in business, you adapt, find new opportunities, and press forward. Many of my competitors offer Pershing and only Pershing, and we don't. We became the first firm in our market to offer a multicustody platform. It's like, many stores sell Coca-Cola exclusively. I don't sell Coke anymore, but now I can sell you Dr Pepper, Fanta, 7UP, etc. As an advisory, we offer more choices now. We offer a niche for people who want something different.

I feel like the company is on more solid footing now. And the culture of the company is still strong. Our human capital is, in fact, the most attractive trait for our new investors. Those who stayed are confident in me because I pulled through. Integrity remains the foundation of what we do. And to me that means doing what you say and saying what you'll do. Congruency between thought, deed, action, and words. It's that simple.

Thoughts on the Industry

Like many people, I am fascinated by the story of the *Titanic*. How could an experienced captain piloting an "unsinkable" behemoth of a ship end up causing history's most notorious nautical disaster? Why was he speeding through the North Atlantic Ocean, which he must have known was ridden with icebergs?

Arrogance is the simple answer. And it provides a lesson for all of us. I was like that captain in some ways, before the walls caved in, thinking that I had seen everything and no one could hustle me. By the time I took over the company, I had been in the industry long enough to know that there were some dirty operators and you had to keep your guard up. I was confident that if any crook ever tried to pull a fast one on me, I'd see it coming from a mile away. I was overconfident in my ability to steer the ship. I never imagined the degree of sophistication and the extent of deception that allowed Biscayne to defraud so many people, a scheme that ensnared not only the direct victims who bought the worthless notes but other people, like myself, who became "collateral damage." I just didn't think it could happen to me.

Now I'm more cautious, humbler. I've seen a lot but probably haven't seen it all. Who knows what other perils are lurking out there in the dark sea? I like to think that, God forbid, if I ever run into a motley crew of bad actors again, I'll be better prepared this time.

At least it hasn't jaded me to the industry as a whole. This industry attracts a lot of energy, talent, and brilliance. Sometimes, it's used for ill; other times, it's used for good. I still believe the good outweighs the bad.

As for the folks who stuck by me, they're doing well. Jerry Schwartz finally retired in September 2021, after thirty-four years at the firm. He's an avid guitar collector, so we gifted him with a vintage guitar as his parting gift.

Myrna is still my right-hand woman. She lives in El Paso, where she is geographically and symbolically positioned to straddle the two markets we serve. She, together with James Gaafar, InSight's chief operating officer, will remain a key part of my leadership team for years to come.

My old professor Federico also resides in El Paso. He's currently working for PNC Bank running the international private banking division and is planning on retiring in the next few years after 20 years with that firm. We're still friends and see each other on occasion.

Nick remains my warrior attorney. Our next big fight is our ongoing lawsuit against Deutsche Bank. We still need to slay that dragon.

And my mother? Thanks for asking. She still full of joy and zest for life and travels as much as she can. I see myself in her and want to be like her when I'm her age.

I intend to prevail on the last remaining arbitrations and, by 2023, I hope to have all black marks on my name from this incident *gone*. A true clean slate.

And how is this for a last laugh? In one final, tie-it-up-with-a-bow stroke of irony, I myself sued InSight.

FINRA maintains a public database (BrokerCheck) of complaints filed against brokers, and even if the complaints against me have been settled, they're still kind of a black mark. So I'm working to get those expunged via FINRA's expungement process. Normally, expungement is designed to allow a broker employed by a firm to clear his or her name. FINRA allows a broker to sue their employer to purge the complaints. My situation is a little unusual in that I'm the owner as well as an employee, but convention never stopped me before. So I formally sued InSight requesting removal of records of arbitrations that have been settled.

Final Lesson

There are a number of lessons to be drawn from this book. The main lesson for me is that we don't know what we're capable of until we give it our all. It's not in good times when we are tested but in crisis.

Of course, in the midst of the crisis, I had doubts. It would have been delusional not to. And sometimes, I even doubted myself. But I never lost *faith* in myself. If I had, I might have folded at the very beginning, the moment I got that termination letter from Pershing.

Instead, I vowed to fight, accepting that I couldn't predict, or control, the outcome but could only give it my all each day.

When I give my best, give my all, the universe responds and shows up. If I'm willing to accept it with humility, own up to my mistakes, be vulnerable, and accept help, there's no dragon too big to slay.

And there is always a Mario willing to lend a helping hand.

TO BE CONTINUED ...

Have you ever found yourself playing poker, and you look around the table and you can't find which player is the fool? If that's the case, most likely, you are the fool. This is the situation in which Deutsche Bank found itself in March 2018.

For years they had been enabling the Biscayne Capital fraudsters to carry out their Ponzi scheme, which by that time had grown to over $300 million, by providing them with all the infrastructure to mint fraudulent securities and sell them to unsuspecting investors.

But now the chickens had come to roost, Deutsche Bank's own creation turned on it, and the Biscayne individuals had overdrafted their account by buying tens of millions of dollars of these fake notes and did not have the money to pay Deutsche Bank.

This is the tale of how one of Europe's most recognizable financial institutions worked with the Biscayne individuals to stick the overdraft onto the account of one of Argentina's wealthiest families and get InSight Securities to pay the bill.

To be continued ...

INSIGHT'S LEGAL TEAM

LEAD LITIGATOR

- Nicholas Iavarone, Esq., Iavarone Law Firm ("Iavarone")

ILLINOIS TEAM

- Laurence Landsman, Esq., Latimer LeVay Fyock LLC ("LLF")
- Sean Rohan, Esq., O'Hagan Meyer ("Ohagan")
- Theodore Peters, Esq., O'Hagan Meyer ("Ohagan")

NEW YORK TEAM

- Karen Ostad, Esq., Globe Advise LLC ("Ostad")
- William Friedman Esq., Gaeta Law Firm ("Gaeta")

FLORIDA TEAM

- Neil S. Baritz, Esq., Baritz and Coleman LLP
- Andrew Thomson, Esq., Baritz and Coleman LLP
- Brad Saxton, Esq., Winderweedle, Haines, Ward & Woodman PA ("WHWW")
- Timothy Kiley, Esq., Winderweedle, Haines, Ward & Woodman PA ("WHWW")
- Andrew Roy, Esq., Winderweedle, Haines, Ward & Woodman PA ("WHWW")
- Jeffrey Deery, Esq., Winderweedle, Haines,

Ward & Woodman PA ("WHWW")

ECUADOR TEAM

- Francisco Estupiñan Barrantes, Fexlaw Abogados ("Fexlaw")

OTHER AREAS OF PRACTICE

- Laurence Elman, Esq., corporate law

- Daniel Legaye, Esq., Legaye Law, regulatory and compliance

- David Anderson, Esq., Anderson Coverage Group LLP, insurance coverage

- Dennis LaGory, Esq., Anderson Coverage Group LLP, insurance coverage

COURT CASES

FINRA ARBITRATIONS

CASE NUMBER	PARTIES	ADVISOR	OPPOSING COUNSEL	INSIGHT COUNSEL
18-02176	Claimants vs. Insight	Hinojosa	McCarthy Lebit	Iavarone/ Ohagan
18-02934	Claimants vs. Insight	Hinojosa	Akerman LLP	Iavarone/ Ohagan
19-03068	Claimants vs. Insight	Hinojosa	Giuliano Law Grp	Iavarone
19-03068	Claimants vs. Insight	Hinojosa	Erez Law	Iavarone
19-00475	Claimants vs. Insight	Haberer	Malecki Law	Ohagan
19-00137	Claimants vs. Insight	Haberer	Malecki Law	LLF
18-02781	Claimants vs. Insight	Haberer	Malecki Law	LLF
21-02265	Insight vs. Respondent	N/A	Cahill, Gordon LLP	Iavarone
20-01432	Insight vs. Respondent	N/A	Ulmer Attorneys	Iavarone

US DISTRICT COURT FOR THE NORTHERN DISTRICT OF ILLINOIS

CASE NUMBER	PARTIES	OPPOSING COUNSEL	INSIGHT COUNSEL
19-cv-02836	Insight vs. Haberer et al.	MPA Law/ Lewis	Iavarone/LLF
18-cv-07572	Insight vs. Edith Hinojosa	Pro Se	Iavarone

19-cv-06343	Insight vs. Amicorp Trustees	Akerman LLP	Iavarone
19-cv-03745	Amicorp Management vs. Insight	Akerman LLP	Iavarone
20-cv-01575	Insight vs. Deutschebank Trust CA	Cahill, Gordon LLP	Iavarone
20-cv-04700	Legaspy vs. FINRA	Pro Se	Iavarone/ Ohagan

US DISTRICT COURT FOR THE SOUTHERN DISTRICT OF FLORIDA

CASE NUMBER	PARTIES	OPPOSING COUNSEL	INSIGHT COUNSEL
20-cv-23864	Insight vs. Deutschebank Trust CA	Cahill, Gordon LLP	WHWW/ Iavarone

FLORIDA MIDDLE BANKRUPTCY COURT

CASE NUMBER	PARTIES	OPPOSING COUNSEL	INSIGHT COUNSEL
19-ap-00323	Insight vs. Edith Hinojosa	Bartolone Law	WHWW

SUPREME COURT OF THE STATE OF NEW YORK

CASE NUMBER	PARTIES	OPPOSING COUNSEL	INSIGHT COUNSEL
654349/19	Deutschebank Securities vs. Insight et al.	Cahill, Gordon LLP	Ostad/LLF

CIRCUIT COURT OF THE 11TH JUDICIAL CIRCUIT FOR MIAMI-DADE COUNTY, FL

CASE NUMBER	PARTIES	OPPOSING COUNSEL	INSIGHT COUNSEL
654349/19	Insight Securities vs. Akerman LLP	Gunster	Iavarone/Baritz

CRIMINAL CASES

- *United States* vs. *Frank Chatburn Ripalda, Case 18-cr-20312, Florida Southern District Court*

- *United States* vs. *Gustavo Trujillo, Case 19-cr-00134, New York Eastern District Court*

- *United States* vs. *Roberto Cortes, Ernesto Weisson, and Fernando Haberer, Case 21-cr-00458, New York Eastern District Court*